The Financially
Intelligent Physician

The Financially Intelligent Physician

What They Didn't Teach You in Medical School

David J Norris, MD, MBA

Dedication

To my wife, Megan, whose perfectly timed question, "Shouldn't you be writing?" helped keep me on task. Her support throughout this process has been invaluable. To my children, Jacob and Adelle, who were very understanding throughout this process. To Tim Zomermaand for being a wonderful friend and encourager. To my friend, Chad Raney, who has encouraged me all along the way, your feedback has been wonderful. To Anthony Singer, thanks for your support. To Mike Flores, the best accounting teacher I will likely ever have. To my Lord and Savior Jesus Christ.

Contents

Part Three—How Healthy Is Your Practice?

Part Four—What are Costs?

Preface

Many years ago I was honored to be given leadership positions within my group. I took the responsibility very seriously and spent many nights concerned about the finances of the group. I was handed financial reports and was expected to make decisions based on the data presented to me. However, I must admit, I wasn't equipped or knowledgeable in reading or understanding these reports. I realized I needed more knowledge—more business experience and education.

This led me to obtain an MBA. During my studies, I discovered a new passion—a mission and purpose, if you will. That mission and purpose is to help my fellow physicians become stronger leaders through business education. This is my attempt to accomplish that mission. This has been a huge goal to accomplish, but the objective will be well worth the time, energy, and money I've spent in this endeavor.

It is my desire that you find value in the following pages. I recognize most physicians cannot return to school for an additional degree in business. I hope I can assist you in becoming more financially literate and better equipped to make improved financial decisions. If you find this information helpful, please don't hesitate to let me know.

Yours in service,
David

Introduction

A physician's practice is like any other small business. Money flows in, and money flows out of the business. You must have more money coming in than going out. Accountants call money coming in revenue and money going out expenses. Revenue is the money made by a practice through its day-to-day activities. For example, it comes from patient visits. It can also come from other sources such as interest or investments. Expenses are the opposite of revenue. An expense is what you've given up to gain something else. Said another way, it's the cost of doing business.

Accounting, like statistics, can be manipulated to whatever point of view the person desires. Numbers can be massaged to influence or deceive the reader. However, a knowledgeable person can quickly find these attempts and uncover the truth. After reading this book, you will have a greater understanding of financial reporting.

Like many entrepreneurs and small business owners, physicians pay very little, if any, attention to their financial reports. They are happy with the money that comes in and think it will last forever. My goal for this book is to give you a solid foundation in understanding financial reports so that you can know how healthy your company or practice is.

It is also important to remember that business owners are not the only people who look at financial reports. If you ever want to get a line of credit, attract investors, or undergo a merger or acquisition, financial reports will be used and studied.

In this book, I will discuss the Big Three financial reports: the Income Statement, Balance Sheet, and Cash Flow Statement. In the following chapters, I will discuss the various ratios and other tests we can use to see just how healthy our practice is. These will yield valuable information and help you make stronger and better financial decisions.

In the second section of the book, we will look at costs and cost accounting. The financial reports will tell you how healthy your practice is, but it is in costing data that you will work to make it better.

The last section of the book has real examples of financial reports that physicians in private practice received from their office managers or staffing companies. These are actual reports given to me by one of my friends who is part of a family practice group. We will look at how to apply what we've learned to real world examples.

As a supplement to this book, I suggest you visit my online educational program at https://learn.davidnorrismdmba.com/. This and my other courses will help you improve your buisness and financial intelligence. If you purchased this book, send an email to support@davidnorrismdmba.com for information about a special discount available to you.

PART ONE

Why Financial Intelligence Matters

1

A Cautionary Tale

A good friend of mine recently shared a story with me. He is a CPA and manages medical practices. Companies usually hire him when they are in deep trouble—the sort of trouble they got themselves into. He feels about it the same way physicians feel when patients ignore their medical conditions and then become very ill. It's not necessarily difficult to stay healthy; all it takes is knowledge and the discipline to use that knowledge. What follows is a story my friend shared with me about one of his clients.

Dr. Joseph Roberts was a cardiologist. He made a good income. Over the past few years, his income hadn't changed much. While he sat with other physicians in the lounge and other social events, he heard them complaining that their costs were rising, revenue was declining, and their income was shrinking. He thought their poor performance had nothing to do with the economy, market, or changes in regulations. He believed it happened to them because they weren't as good as he was. If they were better doctors, he reasoned, then they wouldn't be experiencing financial problems. He continued to earn his level of income because he was an excellent physician, and smart too.

Then a few months later, he received a call from his tax preparer.

"You're broke, you know? Have you considered bankruptcy?" the accountant asked.

Dr. Roberts was shocked. He simply couldn't believe it. How could he be broke? He had been making the same money for the last three years. Nothing had changed as far as he could tell. He didn't understand how he could be broke.

"Well, I've discovered a number of issues. First, there's a difference between the revenue you generate as a physician and what you pay yourself," the accountant replied. "Second, it appears you've some strict terms in your loan agreements that have placed your personal assets at risk as well."

"Whoa, wait, what? How can I be broke if my income hasn't changed? How can I have the money to pay myself if the revenue isn't there?" Dr. Roberts asked.

"Many years ago you set up lines of credit with your bank to cover any gaps you might have between your current expenses and revenue. It would appear that your revenue has declined while your expenses have increased. To cover that gap, you used a line of credit. You borrowed your income for the last three years," the accountant said. "Haven't you been watching your financial statements?"

"Oh sure, I review those every year at tax time. The net profit didn't look like it had changed at all. Are you sure you're right? This is why you got my business instead of the guy I fired last year," Dr. Roberts said.

"Um, okay. How often do you think you should look at those reports? Did you compare them to prior years? Or did you simply look at the bottom line?"

"Once a year should be fine. If the bottom line is okay, everything else is okay."

"That's not true at all. The bottom line is only one report. Did you watch the balance sheet and notice your liabilities were increasing for the last three years?" the accountant asked.

"The balance sheet? No, I only need to focus on the profit and loss statement. That tells me everything I need to know."

He could hear the accountant take a deep breath on the other end of the phone. Dr. Roberts was getting frustrated with accountants telling him how to run his business.

"Dr. Roberts, I know you're a smart man. You do things that help people in dramatic ways. That being said, you need to get a handle on the financial state of your practice. You need to get help and education. It appears that you are bankrupt. Your personal assets are at risk. You need to sit down with an attorney and work out a plan. Hopefully, you'll learn a few things along the way and prevent this from happening to you again in the future. Would you like a few names of some very good attorneys? I can also provide you the name and number of a CPA who specializes in fixing medical practices. I know Don is currently taking on new clients."

"Another accountant? An attorney? I just don't see how what you're telling me is true."

"I'd have a chat with your office manager and previous accountant. They will tell you the same thing I'm telling you. My father once said, 'Just because you're smart in one area doesn't mean you're smart in another. Find out where you're not smart and learn.' Find a good book and learn, Dr. Roberts. And I suggest you give Don Evers a call."

Don eventually became Dr. Roberts's accountant, and the financial reports did, in fact, tell the story of the financial crisis. The problems were plain to see. Over the past three years, Joe's liabilities had risen and risen, and it was apparent on his balance sheet. However, Joe had found it confusing and didn't want to look stupid, so he never asked questions. His real revenue had declined, and his accounts receivable had shot up as well. He was making less money and people owed him more money than ever before. He had used a line of credit to pay his salary. Indeed, his practice was bankrupt.

There are many lessons here. Hopefully, by the time you finish this book, you'll have greater financial intelligence and keep yourself from becoming like Dr. Roberts.

2 | The 4 Ps of Exemplary Patient Care

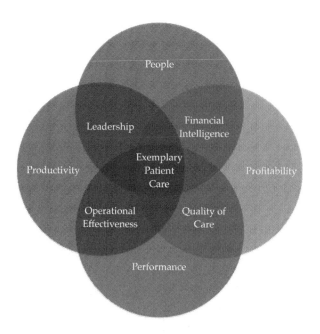

We all want to deliver excellent care to our patients. That's why we went to medical school. We care about people and want to help them. There is a wonderful reward when you're able to help someone else get better. In today's healthcare environment, even though we can get bogged down with EMRs, guidelines, and the like, our goal is still to provide patient care. As a physician leader, your goal, mission, and purpose are to ensure that your organization delivers exemplary patient care. It's an easy thing to say, but it is much more difficult to accomplish.

Exemplary patient care goes beyond the right care at the right time. It encompasses so much more than the therapy. It includes management of all of the resources needed to provide that care. As I began to work with other physician leaders, I developed a model that helps focus attention on four key areas. I call it the Four Ps of Exemplary Patient Care: People, Productivity, Performance, and Profitability.

People

Healthcare organizations are groups of service providers working together to help other people. Their true assets are the people and the knowledge, skills, and judgment their people possess. The ability to diagnose, create a treatment plan, and provide the necessary follow-up to make sure the patient's ailment is properly treated is the service the patient is purchasing from the organization.

Naturally, we desire to find and work with the best, most talented people possible. Unfortunately, it is not always as simple as that. Today, healthcare is delivered as a team, and as a physician leader, you must work diligently to assemble well-functioning teams. The leader is required to understand how and why people behave as they do. You must be able to properly assign tasks and place people in the correct positions. Exemplary patient care only starts with having the right people. The next step is ensuring the highest level of productivity possible.

Productivity

Productivity is the quantity of work performed in a given period. How many phone calls are made in a day? How many patients are seen in an hour? How many bills, or claims, are filed in a day or week?

Strong physician leaders know and understand the many variables that come into play in an active practice. They understand and see how each person's tasks and responsibilities affect and are affected by others within the organization. Physician leaders recognize and work to remove the roadblocks that hinder their people in their daily tasks. You will want to use important tools such as key metrics, benchmarks, scorecards, and other tools as a dashboard to monitor and manage the productivity of the practice in real time where and when it is possible.

Performance

Performance is a measure of the quality of care. Obtaining the right diagnosis at the right time and providing the right therapy at the best possible cost are just pieces of performance. These are more objective metrics you can use to determine the performance of your practice. How the patient feels and what they think is also important when considering performance. Subjective metrics such as patient satisfaction scores give insight into the patients' perception of the service and care provided by the practice. Patient satisfaction scores will become more important as the healthcare industry continues to change. Monitoring your practice's performance will be challenging but necessary.

I think now is a good time to delineate two important yet very different terms as they relate to performance. The first is the treatment (or the therapy) the practice provides. It's the medical side of the equation. Was the diagnosis made correctly? Was the best and most appropriate medical therapy initiated? Did we solve the medical issue or problem the patient is facing? The second is the care provided. Care refers to those aspects related to the customer service side of the equation. How quickly can patients get in to see the physician? How often does the clinic run on time? How nice is the staff? What are the facilities like? Are the bathrooms clean? Frequently, I have spoken with friends who loved their physician but left to find another one not because of poor treatment, but because of poor service or care.

Profitability

Cash flow is of utmost importance to a practice. For the sake of argument, throughout this book, I will assume the physician's salary is included as a part of the expenses of the practice. To keep your doors open and help people, the amount of money coming into the practice must at least equal the amount of money going out. The money going out would include all of the expenses of the practice plus any salary or benefits going to the physician. As a small business owner, your duty is to pay your employees first, and then yourself. Build a budget that includes all of your projected expenses, such as overhead and employee costs, and then add in your own desired salary. If at the end of the year, you have extra cash, you are free to hold on to it for reinvestment into the practice or distribute it to the owners. If you don't have the cash to pay yourself, don't take it from your employees. If you do, it will eventually hurt your practice in many ways. It should go without saying, but you should not set out to lose money. Profitability doesn't just happen. It must be planned.

Losing money makes it very difficult to stay in business and keep the doors open to serve patients. Profitability is not a bad word. It simply means the practice is collecting more than their costs to provide care. If that happens, the practice will have excess cash to pay the physician and acquire newer, more efficient technologies. They have money to invest in the organization and continually improve it by focusing on the people, productivity, and performance.

As a physician leader, you should have a solid foundation in financial intelligence if you are going to make the proper financial decisions. Some might refer to this as business intelligence. However, I feel that business intelligence is much broader than income statements and balance sheets. Business intelligence encompasses process improvement, change management, and leadership.

Exemplary Patient Care

With each decision, the physician leader should think about the Four Ps. They should ask, "Do we have the right people? How well is the team working? What are the roadblocks they face? What can we do to make their jobs more efficient? How can we improve the quality and reduce errors? What capital do we have available to invest? Where is the best place to invest that capital?" Having the right people working as efficiently as possible, doing their best work, and ensuring that your revenue exceeds your costs is the only way to provide exemplary patient care. Once you have all four pieces in place, you are equipped.

Four Characteristics Required for Physician Leader

As the physician leader begins to understand and ingrate the four Ps, they recognize how all four work together to create an environment in which excellent patient care can be delivered.

Leadership

The success of any practice is dependent upon the right people in the right positions having proper leadership skills. People naturally look to you for leadership and guidance. Your employees may bring skillsets and knowledge that impact the effectiveness of the group, but it is your leadership that leverages that knowledge with processes to make the practice productive. A good leader sees what others don't and makes the correct decisions in the face of an ever-changing industry. You must also make hard financial decisions as the practice changes. These important decisions require solid financial intelligence.

Leadership is not only about having the proper business knowledge such as financial intelligence and operational know-how. As a leader, you should be tapped into the culture of the organization. Emotional intelligence gives you the skills to know and understand how your people think and act the way they do. This is incredibly important as we begin to introduce change into the practice.

Operational Effectiveness

The ultimate goal of any practice is to be highly productive while delivering the highest level of care to their patients. This requires that both productivity and performance be closely monitored and managed. Just as we measure and monitor our patients, we need to monitor our practices. Our people being able to help improve the processes is key to a lean and effective practice. Their thoughts, ideas, and efforts are critical. People working at their best (not only their most efficient) is what makes an operation effective. A highly effective operation works to create an environment that maintains the lowest costs thus mitigating the business risks and increasing the probability of profitability.

Quality of Care

The performance of your organization is also critical to profitability. An organization that is delivering quality care works to help maintain the profitability of the practice. Patients will return and recommend others to a practice that consistently delivers the highest quality of care possible. Demand for the practice's services increases and works to help maintain profitability. In turn, the profitability of the practice allows for investment in newer technology, personnel, and other features that ensure the highest quality of performance and care. Having a high-performing practice will help ensure patients are treated with the right therapy at the right time for the right price. This will ultimately raise the value of the practice and its profitability.

Every physician wants their patients to be treated quickly, correctly, and compassionately. Doing so will help the profitability of the practice by raising patient satisfaction, word of mouth referrals, and the general reputation of the practice in the community.

Financial Intelligence

Being profitable is more than simply a positive net income at the end of the fiscal period. A financially healthy practice is the result of the people in the organization and their decisions coupled with the organization's performance. A good physician leader understands that people's decisions affect the practice's profitability. Therefore, it is imperative that those decision makers have a sound and solid understanding of finance and accounting—they need financial intelligence.

Operational effectiveness cannot be accomplished without an understanding of the organization's cost accounting structure. Given the nature of accounting systems in small practices—and healthcare in general—it's probably more appropriate to utilize industry benchmarks to determine your costing structure. As we will see later, most small practices use a cash-based accounting system that makes cost accounting methods difficult, if not impossible, to implement.

When a physician understands and puts into place the Four Ps, the practice is set up to deliver exemplary patient care. When you combine financial intelligence, operational effectiveness, quality of care, and leadership, exemplary patient care is the ideal outcome. Patients are cared for in an efficient, cost-effective, compassionate manner, which is the ultimate goal for any physician.

This Book is About Financial Intelligence

This book addresses one of the most important characteristics of a physician leader. Other books in our series will address the other characteristics of leadership. The objective of this book is to raise your financial intelligence and help you make better decisions so you can deliver exemplary patient care.

3 | Why Do We Care?

Why is financial intelligence important for a physician? Why should we invest our time and energy into being able to interpret these reports? If it was so important, wouldn't they have taught this stuff in medical school?

Unfortunately, the answer is that even though they didn't teach business fundamentals in medical school, this information is incredibly important. I'm not certain why this critical piece is left out of our education. Perhaps it's because of the time it would add to our training, or perhaps our teachers didn't know and understand these concepts. It's difficult to teach what you do not know yourself.

Imagine attempting to make a diagnosis of aortic stenosis without using a stethoscope, ultrasound, or angiography. If all you had to go on was the patient's symptoms, how could you make the diagnosis? How would you diagnose hypertension without measuring their blood pressure? How would you monitor the progress of your therapy? The financial reports provide us with critical information we need to diagnose and treat our practice. The information contained in financial reports is used for a variety of activities and decisions.

One area in which the information is used is the creation and utilization of operational controls. Operational controls are a fancy way of saying plans or actions to be taken to raise revenues, contain or lower costs, and protect the assets of the group. These reports provide information that helps us develop a plan. They also let us know if the plan is working or if it needs to be changed. The costs of the delivery of care must be understood so those costs can be controlled.

The reports also help the group to set and understand their pricing models. Are they billing too little? Are the revenues covering their costs? If not, the members now have information they can use to either lower costs, negotiate higher rates, or both. The more information you have, the better able you are to compare the opportunity costs of a given project or action.

This information is also used for capital procurement options. Investors and bankers study these reports to determine the risk of giving money to the group. How likely is it that the group will pay back the money? How well are they managing the cash they currently have? How efficiently are they using their assets? These and other questions are answered by examining these reports. Later, you will learn to perform these calculations and understand why investors and bankers use these ratios.

4

Mindset

My mentor once said everything in life begins with mindset. He was right. I've discovered that my mindset—my attitude—plays an enormous role in my success.

There are two basic types of mindset: fixed and growth. A fixed mindset says everything in life is fixed. Your talent is fixed. Your abilities are fixed. Your capacity to learn is fixed. The world is fixed. The pie is fixed. Even the "game" is fixed. People with this view see the world in terms of their needs.

A growth mindset is quite different from the fixed mindset. It believes growth is always possible. It sees the potential in things such as your talent, ability, and knowledge. People with this mindset believe they can improve anything they want to. *Want* is the key word. They look at things and want them. They want to help others. They want a successful practice.

Want vs. *need* is a very important distinction. *Need* comes from a fixed mindset and sets into motion a variety of self-talk and thoughts that will bias you or cloud your judgment.

A fixed mindset is not the opposite of a growth mindset. Rather, it's the absence of a growth mindset. Just as darkness is the absence of light and cold is the absence of heat, a fixed mindset is the absence of a growth mindset.

The word that's critical to a growth mindset is *want*. You have to want to improve yourself. You have to want to improve your financial intelligence. I want to help you do just that, but in the end, you must want it for yourself.

Another aspect of the growth mindset that will be very valuable to you throughout this book (as well as your career and even your life) is this: realize you don't have all the answers. You don't know everything and cannot know everything. However, you can know what you do and do not know. Too many times I've seen pride get in the way of a physician's success. They can't or won't accept that they don't understand finances and business. As a result, they wind up making bad decisions and then stubbornly sticking with those bad decisions. They somehow think that if they admit to making a bad decision, they are failures. Please don't do that.

If you have made bad decisions in the past, just realize I'm here to help. Take action and make a decision to correct that bad decision. You can always contact me, and I'll try to help you fix whatever problem you're facing.

We Don't Change Our Glasses, Just Our Hats

How we view money is how we view money. Recently, my real estate agent asked me why so many of the physicians she works with have a hard time coming up with a down payment. At first, I thought she was talking about freshly minted physicians right out of residency. But no, she was talking about physicians who had been practicing for quite some time. I'm not surprised by this, and there is good evidence as to why.

There was a study done in 2009 by Henrik Cronqvist, Professor of Finance in the Department of Finance at the University of Miami. In this study, he showed that CEOs, if left unchecked by a strong board of directors, will take a company's liabilities to whatever level they feel comfortable with in their private lives. According to his research, CEOs who borrowed 100% of the value of their home ran their companies with higher debt ratios. In fact, those ratios were 7.2% higher than those companies whose CEOs had no debt against their personal residence. The bottom line is this: how we view and think about money really doesn't change when we move from one environment to another. We will wear many hats throughout a given day. We might wear a spouse hat, parent hat, program director hat, physician hat, or a volunteer hat. We move from one role to another, changing our "hats." But one thing we rarely change is our glasses. We view the world through the same lenses we wear all day. Sometimes they might get smudged or dirty, but the prescription doesn't change. The purpose of this book is to change your prescription with knowledge.

5

A Word About Your CPA

Recently, Consumer Reports published an issue discussing how safe or unsafe your physician is. Are they on probation? Have they ever been sued? What dark secrets are they keeping from their patients? I'm waiting for a story on accountants and how they aren't all equal in their ability. Until then, I'll write this book for you.

Accountants, like physicians, are supposed to act according to a code of conduct and ethics. They are to be knowledgeable and competent. Your CPA or accountant has taken classes and passed an exam. The initials, CPA, after their name mean they are a certified public accountant. It does not mean that what information they give you is certified. This distinction is very important. Just like with physicians, there are good physicians, and there are physicians who shouldn't practice medicine.

Your CPA is an expert, but don't always trust them. Ask lots of questions. Always ask for information they don't have. If they can't or won't give it to you, find another CPA. Many times physicians will ask each other whom they would recommend as a CPA for their practice. Colleagues might not be the best source of information on this topic. Instead, ask a trusted banker or attorney. These professionals tend to work with CPAs a lot and are likely to know which ones to avoid. It's your practice, your career, your livelihood on the line. Take action to protect it.

Allow me to make a quick comment on selecting an attorney or accountant. Don't just use your buddy or the spouse of a friend. You should thoroughly examine the professional and make certain they are experienced in dealing with physician practices and healthcare issues in general. You do not want them learning on your dime.

What Your Accountant Should Be Doing: Accounting Principles and Concepts

Accounting, like any profession, has fundamental principles and concepts that are universally applied regardless of the industry or business type. These concepts are very important to keep in mind when examining a firm's financial statements.

Generally Accepted Accounting Principles

Generally Accepted Accounting Principles (GAAP) were created so that different companies would have a standard way to report their finances to the general public. This was to provide the investor a minimum level of consistency in the financial statements when they are considering investing opportunities. GAAP consist of standards set by policy boards and commonly accepted practices in accounting. It outlines things such as the appropriate method of recognizing revenue, what items should appear on a balance sheet, and how to report financial data.

Materiality

Materiality relates to the significance of an amount, a transaction or discrepancy. It involves how important or how large of an impact a transaction or accounting practice has on the financial decision-making of the leaders and investors of the firm. As a manager, you will need to help determine what is material and what is not.

Periodicity

Periodicity is based upon the assumption that business activities can be divided into measurable intervals. All business activity is dynamic. It constantly changes over time. Revenues and expenses fluctuate with each period whether it is a day, week, month, or year.

Matching

The matching principle is one of the basic underlying guidelines in accounting. It directs a company to report an expense on its income statement in the same period as its related revenues. Said another way, it requires you to report your expenses in the same time period as your revenue. In accrual accounting, this means that expenses should be recorded during the period in which they are incurred regardless of when those activities yield revenue. Revenue is recognized when the goods or services are sold (the contract is signed, or case is delivered). This doesn't mean you actually got paid for providing goods or services, and it doesn't mean you paid cash out to your debtors.

Under the cash basis method of accounting, expenses are recognized and booked when the expense was actually paid. Revenue is recognized when the cash is received. If cash comes into your business or leaves your business, then you record the transaction in the general ledger.

The good thing about accrual accounting methods is that the expenses generated by a practice are matched to the revenue they helped generate. With a cash basis system, expenses and revenues can become uncoupled and cost accounting efforts can get quite difficult. This is especially true when our days in accounts receivable, a measure of how long it takes to get your money, can exceed 75 days in some settings.

This is a vital concept to master so you can accurately interpret financial reports.

Accounting Entity

This principle assumes that the business *entity* is a complete and separate entity from the *owners* of the business entity. If you have more than one business, each company keeps separate books and bank accounts. Those accounts are also separate from your personal accounts. There is to be no commingling of funds.

Going Concern

This principle assumes that a firm will continue to exist long into the future and will meet its obligations and fulfill its commitments. It also assumes the firm will not liquidate the assets in the foreseeable future. This principle allows for accused or deferred transactions, such as prepaids, to be recognized in future accounting periods per the matching principle.

Consistency

This principle states that once an accounting method is utilized by a firm, it will continue to be used throughout the life of the firm. If a change is made, full disclosure and explanation for the change must be given. You will want to know and understand the underlying assumptions being made by those who create your financial statements. These are not typically disclosed on internal financials, which are most of the reports you will see on a regular basis. If you don't know, then ask. If they can't answer, find someone else to do the job.

Conservatism

The conservatism principle is a concept of recognizing expenses as soon as possible when uncertainty exists. It also states revenues and assets should be recognized when it is reasonably certain they will be collected. If there is uncertainty about a loss, the loss should be booked. If there is uncertainty about a gain, the gain should not be recognized. This is an important principle and required by the GAAP.

Historical Costs

When a practice acquires an asset, the cost at the time of purchase is recorded. Even if the asset has increased in value, such as a building and land, the historical cost is maintained on the books. Yet we can depreciate (an estimated loss of value due to ordinary wear and tear) the asset over the life of the asset. Why can we depreciate an asset but not appreciate it? It's simple: we know what we paid for the asset. That number is firm and identifiable. Appreciation is more nebulous and involves educated guesswork. Accountants are taught that guesswork is bad, bordering on evil. This goes back to the principle of conservatism. Because of this, accountants will use the cost of an asset rather than the market value. Things can get sketchy quickly if you begin to record an assumption on the value of the asset. If you do, you might think that you're worth more than you are. This might lead you to take risks you might not be able to afford.

When to Get a Second Opinion

You and your accountant or office manager have a nice relationship. You trust them. You think they do a good job. How do you know that for certain? Is there somewhere you can go to see how well ranked your accountant really is? Not really. What are you to do then? Sometimes it is a good idea to get a second opinion. Have someone else look at your business and books. This is recommended particularly if you cannot get straight answers from whoever is managing your books. If something doesn't add up, get another expert involved. Go out and hire an outside firm or CPA to fully audit your books. Of course, as with any decision, there are pros and cons.

Pros

Perhaps one of the best thing about getting an external audit is that you get a second pair of eyes looking at your books and business. Maybe they will discover something you've missed or had not thought of. Get a firm that deals with practices similar to yours. They will be able to tell you what has been successful for other practices. They will also be able to ask the right questions. Sometimes those questions are hard for you to ask, so having someone else ask them can ease the pain of the question.

Using an outside source, you get someone who has no real interest other than giving you a solid report and picture of your company. They do not know the politics of the office. They lack all of the historical baggage that your office carries with it every day. They are able to be clear in their vision and honest in their reports.

You can also consider an internal audit and let your people review their own work. It's cheaper, but an internal audit might fail to discover fraud, depending on who is doing the fraud.

Cons

No one likes being audited, even accountants. They might feel like they are not trusted or are being second-guessed. It might irritate your people. Their feelings might be hurt just like ours might be when a patient gets a second opinion from another physician. It is also nice when the other physician gives similar advice. The same thing will happen with your people

It will cost money too. Accountants aren't always inexpensive. Getting an external firm or CPA to do an audit will cost cash. Internal audits cost less, but there probably is a reason why you're contemplating an external audit. If you suspect fraud or poor accounting practices, you'll have to decide if the cost of an external audit is worth discovering the truth.

The Biggest Reason for an External Audit: Theft

Embezzlement is a frequent problem for any business, and medical practices are no exception. In fact, it might be easier for embezzlement, or misappropriation of funds, to occur in a medical practice because the owners lack some of the fundamental business knowledge needed to recognize it when it happens. Strong internal controls and checks should be in place not only to prevent embezzlement but to monitor for performance and productivity issues.

Here is a list of items that might be warning signs of misappropriation of funds in a medical practice.

- Decreasing cash to total current assets
- Flat or declining sales with an increasing cost of sales
- A/R increasing compared to cash
- Slower posting of A/R payments
- Increasing patient billing and payment complaints
- Increasing soft expenses (such as consulting, advertising, food, and beverage, etc.)
- Reclassification of line item expenses (This trick makes horizontal analysis more challenging.)
- New or unusual vendors appearing in reports
- Bad debt write-offs increasing

To prevent embezzlement, you should work with knowledgeable and trusted vendors or employees to establish safeguards. You should demand consistency in the reporting of the financial reports and metrics. Any change in the reporting should be signed off by you and only after you understand and agree with the change. Bad debt write-offs should be approved by you or someone you trust.

Don't be afraid to ask for an external audit if you suspect something is amiss in your books. Even though your accountant might be offended, it's better to know if there is an issue than to have someone steal from you. If nothing if found, you know you can trust the accountant. If something is found, you discover who is doing what, and if the accountant isn't complicit, they now know what they might have overlooked.

6

Cash is King

It's been said that cash is king. If you listen to investment analysis on CNBC or Bloomberg, they almost always discuss cash in their analysis of a company. Why? Because it's true: cash is king. Understanding cash, how and where it flows in your practice, is key to understanding the viability of your practice. How many companies have we heard of on the news that went bankrupt despite having wonderful sales? Why did this happen? They went bankrupt because they failed to control their cash. If you cannot understand or know where your cash is coming from or going to, then you have no hope of controlling it.

By reading and studying your financial reports, you can begin to understand and control your cash. Businesses go bankrupt when they run out of cash—period. You can run out of cash for a variety of reasons. First, poor or low sales, or—in our case—poor or low volume and procedures. Second, the practice might not be competent in collecting what they have billed and are owed. Third, the practice's or group's costs are too high and exceed the revenue. Finally, your debt and other liabilities become too large, and the monthly payments eat into your cash or consume it all. All three of these scenarios can be seen and predicted if you know how to read financial reports. By the end of this book, you should have a better idea of how to do just that.

Financing Your Practice (Capital Structure)

There are three basic sources of cash or capital for a practice when you're starting out or need cash in a pinch. Understanding financial reports will help you know which source is best for your particular situation. The three sources are owner financing, investors, and debt servicing.

Owner financing is where the owner of the practice puts their own cash into the deal or practice. They either contribute cash or leverage their personal assets and then use that cash in the practice. The cash owners put into the practice can either be structured as an equity contribution or as a loan to the practice. Each option has benefits and risks. You should speak with your accountant and attorney to make certain you are fully aware of the risks and benefits so that you aren't surprised later.

Investors can be anyone who is willing to give you money. They trust you and believe they will earn a return on their money. Sometimes all they want is a return. However, don't be surprised if they ask for a little more control, especially if the check they write you is substantial. You will have to decide what risk to benefit ratio is comfortable for you. Equity means ownership. Ownership means control and decision-making responsibilities. How that decision-making process is structured is very important. Consult with your attorney before you begin to issue stock to someone. Know what you're willing to give up and what the cost will be if you take someone's money. Just watch a few episodes of Shark Tank, and you will know exactly what I'm talking about.

Debt servicing simply means you borrow money from someone. It could be a bank, friends, family members, or whoever else you can convince to give you money. They don't have any control of your company. Typically, the lender requires you to personally guarantee the loan, provide collateral, and/or have a claim to the assets of the practice such as computers, accounts receivable, etc. That shouldn't happen because you borrowed the money based upon a solid business plan, and you have the highest level of integrity.

7

Timing is Everything

As with most things in life, timing matters. This is especially true when it comes to accounting. It's also important to know when you recognize the revenue you receive for goods or services provided. If you're using an accrual-based method, the cash flow statement is critical to understanding where the money is coming from. With a cash-based system, you'll have a better feel for how much cash you've got, but you won't be able to match the revenue to expense.

Let's consider a practice modeled on the clinic of a friend of mine. We'll call it Physicians of America (POA). Let's say they open a second clinic, and it's going gangbusters. They did their analysis, studied the market, and decided to open the second office in an underserved area of town. Patients are filing into their offices. Great, right?

Well, maybe not. Remember, the charges/revenues are being generated, but the receipt of cash hasn't occurred yet. That will take a few months. Yet, during the first few months of operation, they will have expenses. The power company wants to be paid as does the water department, the phone company, the EMR provider, not to mention all of their employees.

That's why the leaders of POA need to watch the income statement and balance sheet closely. They need to make certain that they have enough cash on hand to pay for all of the expenses they are incurring. If the clinic doesn't receive their money in time, they could run out of cash. Miss a few bills, and they could go broke, and the lenders and contractors want their money. Worse yet, the owners might have personally guaranteed the loans for the expansion. If they did that, then their personal assets could be at risk as well.

Remember GAAP? The matching principle is critical and will be addressed next.

A Tale of Two Accounting Methods

There are two types of accounting methods: cash basis and accrual basis accounting. There are differences between these two methods, and only one meets the GAAP standards.

Cash Basis

When the cash basis of accounting is used, income is recorded when it's received, and expenses are recorded when they are paid. Whenever cash comes into or leaves the company, the transaction is recorded. Typically, this method of accounting does not account for any receivables (money you're owed) or payables (money you owe).

An example would be Dr. King sees a patient in January. If they collect a $30 copayment at the time of the visit, the $30 would be recorded as income for the month of January. Then the billing cycle begins. The claim is submitted to the payer. They wait for their money. Maybe the claim is denied, or the payer has "technical" issues and pays the bill of $100 in February.

On a cash basis accounting method, the cash from the payer would be recorded as $100 of income in February. The big disconnect is that the expenses incurred in January were paid and recorded on the income statement for January, yet the bulk of the income generated in January would be reported in February. This violates the matching principle of the GAAP.

Cash accounting is less complex and easier to do from a book-keeping process. That's why most small businesses use this method. All they are doing is keeping track of the cash flowing in and out of your business. Cash is king, and you need to keep track of your cash, but using a cash basis method has some serious drawbacks. First, it violates the GAAP principle of matching. It's probably a good idea to know what it costs you to see a patient or what you earn from each payer. With the cash-based system, your expenses and income are "uncoupled." Second, it doesn't give you an accurate picture of your financial health. It doesn't keep track of receivables and payables. You might use a modified cash basis system and track your accounts receivable, but you still will not get a clear picture of what is going on financially.

Accrual Basis

The accrual basis of accounting is the opposite of the cash method. With an accrual method, income and expenses are recorded when the work is actually done, not when the cash comes in or leaves. This method allows you to match your work with your revenue and expenses.

Let's suppose Dr. King uses an accrual method of accounting. She sees a patient in January. They collect a $30 copayment, submit a claim for $100, and pay their people. The accountant would record the total of the visit, $130, as income in January. $30 would post to cash, and $100 would be held in accounts receivable. The expenses of seeing the patient would also be recorded in January. If she pays her people $100 to help her with the visit, then $100 will be booked as an expense in the same period as the income.

This method of accounting gives you a more realistic picture of your practice's financial health. It also meets the GAAP standard of matching.

There are drawbacks to the accrual method, however. It is more complex and costlier to implement. It also doesn't track the flow of cash very well. If you want to see where your cash is flowing to and from, then a third financial report must be created: the cash flow statement. If the proper accounting systems are not in place, then you could show high revenues yet be broke with no cash. Don't let that point keep you from using the accrual method though as it is superior and will give you better information for cost controls down the road.

Which One to Use

As a small business owner, deciding which one to use should be one of the first questions you ask your accountant. The cash method is simple and straightforward and will provide you information on how much cash you have right now. The accrual method is more complex, and more effort is needed to do it correctly. There are certain times when the IRS or SEC will require you to use the accrual method. Also, some small businesses use a hybrid method of accounting, using cash for income and expenses and accrual for inventory, receivables, and payables. I would suggest you speak with your accountant to learn more. The important lesson is to know what you might be missing if you use a cash basis accounting system.

8 | Accountant-Speak: Some Important Financial Terms

Words have meanings, and in healthcare, we are very specific in the words we use when communicating with each other. "They've got something wrong with their heart" is quite different than saying, "The patient has an ischemic cardiomyopathy," or, "They have severe mitral valve regurgitation with a flail leaflet." Accountants are the same with their lexicon.

Revenue

Revenue is the money a company earns through the sale of goods, services, rents, and other sources such as investments and income from dividends. It's the top line number—the money that comes into the company. It is not profit. It also shouldn't be confused with cash flow. Revenue can be received by the company in either cash or as a receivable, e.g., credit extended to the customer.

Expense

These are the costs associated with the activities of the company. They are the costs of doing business. Expenses include raw materials, labor costs, and non-cash items such as credit purchases and depreciation of the assets held by the company. Expenses represent money leaving the company so the company can operate and earn revenue.

Profit

Simply put, profit is revenue minus expenses. Often *earnings* is used as a synonym of profit. There are different profit metrics one can use. Gross profit, net profit, earnings before interest, taxes, depreciation, and amortization (EBITDA) are just a few of the profit metrics I will discuss later. When someone says their proposal will be profitable, just realize that there are many different types of profit. Ask them which one they mean when they say profit and what assumptions they have put into the numbers.

Asset

An asset is anything owned by the company that has value. This can be physical (cash, real estate, equipment, stocks), or a claim on a debt (the money you're owed, as in accounts receivable). They might also be patents. An important aspect of the asset is its liquidity—how quickly it can be converted into cash. Current assets are those assets that can be converted into cash quickly. In accounting, *quickly* refers to within one year. Long-term assets are those assets that cannot be liquidated or converted into cash in less than one year. Other classifications of assets are physical, financial, and intangible assets. Intangible assets are things like brand names, know-how or knowledge, and goodwill.

Liability

A liability is a financial obligation. In other words, it's debt. The company owes money to someone. It's a future claim against the company by another entity or person. Just like with assets, liabilities are either current or long-term liabilities. It's either due and must be paid in less than one year, or the terms of debt allow for a longer payback period.

Cost of Goods Sold

In the manufacturing world, the term cost of goods sold (COGS) is widely used. However, in the service industries, this concept gets a bit sketchier. Some people will still refer to the cost of services rendered as COGS, while others may say cost of services sold (COSS), production cost, or the cost of sales or revenue.

It's important to get an idea of what goes into the number. With manufacturing, it is usually cleaner and easier to arrive at this number than with service industries. In an attempt to explain this concept, I'll begin with manufacturing and then introduce the service side.

In manufacturing industries, COGS is the total cost of making the company's products. It's the raw material, labor costs, and parts costs. If an employee's time and energy or raw materials went into the product, then that cost gets lumped into this number. COGS typically doesn't include other overhead expenses such as advertising, shipping, and other indirect costs such as administrative costs. COGS is important because it is the number we will use to calculate the gross margin.

In service industries such as IT or healthcare, you might see the term cost of services used instead. The principle remains the same, though. Items that would be included in the cost of services number are the raw materials you use to create your service. Direct Labor would also be included in the number. This is the salary or wages you pay the people who are doing the service. (In Part 4, we will dig deeper into this concept.) A good rule of thumb in determining what to include in the cost of revenue number is to ask, "What will it cost me today if I don't make this sale?" or, "Does this cost only occur when the services are sold or delivered?" If the answer is yes, then it goes into cost of services. Another question might be, "Does this cost go up and down as the sales of service go up and down?" If yes, then it is part of the cost of service number.

Operating Expense

This is the company's expenses related to the production of their goods and services. It includes things like wages paid for employees, research and development, and raw materials. It might seem like it's the same as COGS, but it's not. COGS is like a warehouse full of inventory. Operating expense is the cost of running the daily activities of the business. Another way of looking at it is this: if you had no sales, you would have no costs of goods sold, but you would still have expenses to keep your doors open.

Operating Profit

This is the revenue the company gets from its regular activities less the costs of doing business. It is revenue minus everything but tax and interest.

Equity

This is an ownership interest in the firm. It's what is left over if all of the assets were sold and liabilities were paid. It's good if this number is positive and not so good if it's negative.

Current Asset/Liability

Current assets and liabilities are those that can be either converted to cash or are due in less than one year. It's important to separate short-term and long-term assets and liabilities into these two categories when we get into the financial health of the company. It becomes very important when considering the impact of cash flow, as I will discuss later in this book.

Contractual Adjustments

Contractual adjustments are the negotiated rates the third party payers pay you for your services. They are the values you and the payer have agreed upon. The payer might be private insurance companies, the government, or whoever else is responsible for paying for your services. You might bill $10 for a service, but the payer will want a discount or have a target number, so you would negotiate your fee which might be $7. Your adjustment would then be $3 or 30%.

Debits and Credits

You might have heard these terms before. Most likely it is associated with your debit card and credit cards. However, you should probably forget what you think you know about these terms. Depending upon the account type—liability or asset—a debit may increase or decrease the balance of the account. The same thing occurs with credits. It has to do with what is known as the double-entry accounting method.

Let's use a purchase of office equipment as an example. You might pay cash for the waiting room furniture. You would decrease your cash account and increase your property and equipment account. Since equipment is an asset, debits increase their balances. The transaction must also have a credit to balance it out on the books. So a credit would be posted to your cash account, decreasing the balance. It would look something like this.

Figure 1.1 – Debit and Credit Example

Account	Debit	Credit
Office Equipment	$2,500	
Cash		$2,500

If you remember the accounting equation, you can easily figure out what a debit will do to an account. Assets = Liabilities + Equity. Debits increase the balance of assets. Credits will decrease the balance of liabilities and equity accounts.

PART TWO

The Big Three

9

A True Story

I am not like most physicians—I enjoy looking at the numbers. I find it fun to pour over them and spot trends. Financial reports are intriguing and exciting. They are also necessary if you are going to have a healthy practice. My love for these reports isn't as contagious as I would like.

A friend of mine asked me to review the financial reports from his group. I was more than happy to help him learn about finance and accounting. It's exciting to help others grow as business leaders. We met at a local coffee shop one rainy morning. It was one of those nice, cool, light rains. Not too hard yet not an annoying drizzle either. He waved as I walked into the shop.

"Good morning, Bill! How are you this morning?" I said as I sat down with my cup of coffee in hand.

"Good, David. Thanks for meeting me. I'm looking forward to learning about these reports," he said.

After some small talk about our families, practices, and hobbies, we got down to work.

"Let me see what you've got," I said.

He handed me a stapled packet of paper with maybe ten sheets of paper. The first three pages were a typed executive summary of the practice's performance for the last month. It was a nice summary and something that might be useful, but I wanted to look at the real reports. I turned to page four, the productivity report. Interestingly, they presented operational data first. That's fine, I guess, I thought to myself. The report was fairly standard. It showed the revenue from their main office and two satellite offices. The expenses allocated to each center were listed. The bottom line was positive for two centers and negative for one office. Below the net income line was the allocation of labor and overhead as a percentage of the total overhead and labor. I made a note of that and moved on.

I flipped over to the income statement. Now we were getting somewhere. The report included seven columns. The left-hand column contained the line items. The next two columns were for the month of May of the current year, and the month of May of the previous year. The fourth column was the variance between those two columns. The same was repeated for the year-to-date of the current year, year-to-date of the previous year, and the variance between the two. I was pleased to see this, as it can be very informative in doing financial analysis.

"This seems good. Now, I'm going to ask some questions, and I don't want you to get upset. These are just questions to get you thinking. I don't expect you to have the answers—yet," I said. I held my breath waiting for Bill's reply.

"Yeah, I'm not entirely sure what I'm looking at, but I know I need some help. So fire away."

"Ok. I like the horizontal analysis I see here. That's helpful. But my questions are about these line items. Under physician expenses, what is "communication"? What goes into that number? Do you know? And how is that different from the communications line item in your general and administrative section?"

"I don't know. But I'll find out," Bill said as he began to jot down some notes.

"Under your nursing expenses, you've got a line item titled nurses salary and nurses salaries salary. What is that? How are those two different? Do you know?" I asked Bill.

"No, I don't."

"Ok, no problem," I said as I took a sip of my coffee. "Let's continue. I see a management fee. Do you know what they charge you? Is it a flat fee? A percent of monies collected or billed? I also see a new item, collection fees. In the previous year column, its balance is zero, but so far this year it's almost $35,000. Do you know what it is?"

There was silence except for the sound of lead scratching across paper as Bill wrote some comments. He then looked up at me and said, "No."

This went on for about another ten minutes. After we had covered the three pages of the income statement, I flipped to the next section of the report. It was a payer mix report, nicely organized, a necessary report. The next page was a days-in-accounts-receivable report. It showed a good trend, or least a trend that made it appear the billing company was doing a good job.

"Do you know how many bills they simply write off or ignore? Are they just dropping some really old bills to make that number in days in A/R over 180 as small as possible?"

"I've no idea," Bill said.

The next few pages were utilization reports such as patients seen per office site and the hours of operation of each site. It was good information for planning, but there was no historical data to compare it to. All it showed was the month of May. I decided to stop asking some questions and ask if Bill wanted another cup of coffee or doughnut. When we decided to return to the issue at hand, I asked Bill for the rest of the reports.

"What do you mean? This is what we are given at the meetings," Bill said.

"Wait, what? Where is your balance sheet? I need to see your balance sheet."

"Balance sheet? What's a balance sheet? I don't know that I've ever seen one of those in the report packet."

"A balance sheet shows what you own and what you owe. It's critical. How much cash do you have in the bank right now? That's on the balance sheet. That's important, particularly when payroll rolls around. What do you owe and to whom? Have you borrowed money? Are your liabilities growing or shrinking? What are you guys doing with your cash? Paying down debt? Paying yourselves bonuses? Investing in assets? The balance sheet will tell you things, Bill. Without it, you're really only getting half of the picture.

"The income statement is valuable, but it's just one part of the story. It's like listening to patients' heart tones. You can tell if their rhythm is normal and maybe if there might be some valve disease. But if you want more information, you need to dig deeper. You might order an EKG of a patient. That will tell you about the electrical activity of the patient's heart and if they might have areas of concern. The next step might be an echo or a trip to the cath lab. The point is, we don't usually rely on just one data point, one exam. We dig deeper. That's why we need to have at least the income statement and balance sheet. The operational data is important too, and we will use when we make an operational and financial decision."

I explained how the income statement and balance sheets are related, how you can make money yet go bankrupt, and how to make financial decisions on opening or closing an office. After another few cups of coffee, Bill thanked me, and we left. That's when I decided to write this book. He had some information, but he didn't know what it was or how to use it. That's the purpose of this book. To help you begin to understand how to interpret these reports and when to ask questions. Two basic questions should always be in the front of your mind when looking at these reports: What is this, and why is it here?

10 | The Big Three

There are three basic financial reports any business owner should review on a monthly basis. These are the income statement, balance sheet, and statement of cash flow. In Part 2, we will discuss what items appear on which report as well as some important ratios that will help you determine the financial health of your practice.

It's important that you become familiar with these statements. You will want to know what appears on each report and why. Just like with an arterial blood gas or basic metabolic profile, these reports will inform you of the health of your company. Once you know that, you can develop a treatment plan to correct any present or future problems.

Three Basic Questions

If we run a practice or clinic (or any business unit), there are three basic questions we should ask:

1. How much money came in?
2. Where did the money go?
3. How much money is left?

There isn't a crystal ball we can use to answer these three questions. Instead, we must rely on humans and their accounting systems to gain insight into these questions. We can find the answers by studying financial reports.

Later in this book, when we examine the financial health of a company and ratio analysis, we will ask three similar questions:

1. Is the company profitable? Are we making money?
2. Are we able to pay our bills? Do we have enough money to pay our bills?
3. Is our equity growing or shrinking?

In the next section, we will examine three financial reports in detail and examine methods we can use to check our practice's health. Each report is a piece of the puzzle, and we should look at all three to get a good picture of our practice.

11

Revenue Cycle

In Parts 2 and 3 of this book, I will discuss financial statements, ratios, some financial decision-making, and cost accounting. But let's first look at the process of billing and collecting, or what is referred to as the *revenue cycle*.

The revenue cycle has multiple steps, making it easier for the process to break down and items to go overlooked. Some of these steps possess a component of patient contact while others are completed in the back office. Information about the patient will be passed along from one person or department to another. Hand-offs are dangerous because that's where errors can occur. In my next book, I will give you a solid system and process to monitor and improve any process or system in your practice.

The Revenue Cycle

Scheduling the Appointment

The first step in the revenue cycle is when the patient contacts your office to schedule an appointment. It might be the patient themselves or another physician's office contacting your practice. You will need to think about who will be making appointments for you and how they do it. Will you use the phone only, or will you also use an online method? If you use more than one method, be aware of how these methods are sharing information.

This is one of the most important steps in generating revenue in the current fee-for-service system. We get paid for seeing patients. As the system changes to quality outcomes, scheduling will still be important because it will be related to patient satisfaction. Examine your scheduling system today and see where you can improve it. Assuming you want to grow, examine your system from the perspective of the patient and your referral sources, not the owners or the physicians of the clinic. Develop the attitude that both sources are your customers, and make it easy for them to see you.

Registration:
Collecting Insurance, Payment, and Demographic Data

The next step is registration. This is collecting and verifying the payment information of the patient. It's critical to have accurate information, especially if third-party payers are involved. Payers seem to look for any reason to deny a claim which leaves you holding the bag and providing free service. Having a strong system that ensures this important data is collected correctly at the very beginning will only help to reduce your claims denials.

The Patient Encounter

Once you have all of the patient's information, a chart is assembled or retrieved. Your staff puts the patient in an exam room and collects the necessary data points, such as the chief complaint, weight, vitals, etc. Then you do the work you love—taking care of patients. The encounter needs to be documented properly. Accurate documentation is important for the proper coding of the visit. If you do your own coding, then make sure your documentation of the visit supports your coding level. If you don't perform your own coding, make it easy for your coders with full and complete documentation.

Coding the Visit and Charge Capture

Either you or a coder will look at your notes and generate the proper evaluation and management (E&M) codes for the visit. This information is then passed along to third-party payers. You will find it helpful to periodically review with your coders what information is needed for the various E&M codes. Sometimes it can be confusing how to code the visit, especially if the patient is complex. Remember, what seems straightforward to us isn't always straightforward to others. It's in your best interest to ensure coding can be completed quickly and accurately so the charge can be created and then submitted to the payers promptly. Many third-party insurance companies have time requirements for filing claims. Any non-clean claim received after a specified time period may not be eligible for payment, and you might be contractually barred from billing the patient. If that happens, then you have just provided free care.

Claim Submission

The next step is to submit your claim to the payers. These days, most claim submissions are completed electronically. In fact, some payers require electronic filing. Periodically, review how quickly your claims are being submitted and look for ways to improve the process if possible.

Follow-up

This step is probably the most painful for your office staff. They must check each claim and see whether or not the claim has been paid or not. Furthermore, they must verify whether the proper amount was paid. If the payment is late or for the wrong amount, they have to speak with the payer. This can be time-consuming and draining. Be aware of how hard they are working for you to get your money, and show appreciation and gratitude for their hard work.

12

The Income Statement

The income statement, or profit and loss (P&L) statement, is a useful tool for evaluating the performance of a company for a specific period, usually one month. It might also be labeled as an operating statement, statement of earnings, or earnings statement. The point is that this is a report that shows how much the company made and how much it spent over a given period. These reports summarize the revenues and expenses the firm recognized for that given period. It reports the *net income*, or *bottom line*: how much money is left over from sales activity after all the bills have been paid.

Also be aware of other words in the title of the report. Sometimes they might say *actual* or *pro forma*. Be wary if you see pro forma—that means it's just someone's best guess. A pro forma is a projection, an estimated guess based upon a set of given assumptions. There's nothing wrong with using a pro forma, but you should always know what assumptions were made while building the report. It might simply be someone's vision of the future—a rainbows-and-sunshine report. I'm not saying it's bad to be optimistic, but a pinch of pessimism can save you money. Always question the assumptions that go into creating the report.

For a physician's practice, *revenue* would be all the revenue generated from professional fees (seeing patients) and other income from laboratory testing, radiology exams, and the like. Expenses would include employee wages and benefits, inventory and supplies used, overhead, etc. Figure 2.1 illustrates the basic components of an income statement. Figure 2.2 is an example of a general income statement. It's more of what you're likely to receive from your accountant or office manager. In Figure 2.3, we see the actual income statement for Physicians of America.

Figure 2.1 - General Income Statement

Income Statement for *Period of Time*

	Gross Sales
-	Adjustments
=	Net Sales
-	Cost of Goods Sold
	Raw Materials
	Overhead
	Depreciation
=	Gross Profit
-	Sales, General, & Administrative
=	Operating Income
-	Interest Expense
=	Pretax Income
-	Income Taxes
-	Special Items & Extraordinary Expenses
=	Net Income

Figure 2.2 - Sample Medical Practice Income Statement

Medical Practice USA

Income Statement

For Year Ending Dec 31, 20XX

Revenues

+	Professional Fees
+	Other Types of Fees
+	Drug Fees
=	**Total Gross Fees**
+	Adjustments & Refunds
=	**Total Revenue**
-	Physician Expenses
-	Non-physician Expenses
-	Staff Expenses
-	General & Administrative Expenses
=	**Net Income**

Figure 2.3 - Physicians of American Income Statement

Income Statement
December 31, 2014

Gross Charges

Professional Service Charges	1,139,223
Orthopedic Charges	9,101
Injection Charges	101,941
Immunization Charges	147,206
Procedure Charges	115,860
Laboratory Charges	728,329
Radiology Charges	122,113
Hospital Charges	84,383
Nursing Home Charges	20,061
Miscellaneous Charges	3,375
Gross Charges Total	2,471,593
Contractual Adjustments	-1,121,820
Net Medical Charges	1,349,773
Capitation Revenue	121,245
Other Operating Income	65,262
Adj to Cash Collections	259,478
Total Net Revenue	1,795,757

Expenses

Total Personnel Expense	599,496
Total Computer Expense	21,929
Total Radiology Expense	28,984
Total Laboratory Exp	89,068
Total Building Exp	232,875
Total Supplies Expense	114,888
Total Operating Expenses	1,087,240
Total Furn / Equip Exp	7,684
Total Purchased Svcs	29,845
Total EE Related Svcs	22,016
Total Gen & Adm Exp	41,272
Non-Op Rev/Exp	71,493
Total Overhead	172,310
Total Expenses	1,259,550
Net Profit	536,207

The income statement starts with net sales or revenue. In the case of a medical practice, it would be net charges. Net charges are the final charges you collect from a payer after you apply the contractual write-offs. Contractual write-offs occur when a medical practice executes a payer agreement with a third-party payer like United HealthCare (UHC).

The UHC agreement stipulates you will accept 125% of the current Medicare fee schedule ($100) for reimbursement for all services provided. However, your current standard fee schedule is structured at 200% of the current Medicare fee schedule. In this example, the medical practice would generate and average a contractual write-off of 37.5% per item charge under this agreement.

$$\frac{\$200 - \$125}{\$200} = \frac{\$75}{\$200} = 37.5\%$$

In the case of POA, we see what their contractual write-offs are for each provider in Figure 2.4. When this data is compared with their total charges for each provider, we can see what type of discount they are giving to each third-party payer.

Figure 2.4 - Physicians of America Write-offs Report

Contractual Adjustments:

Other Contractual Adjustments	$	(65,177)
Aetna Adjustments	$	(19,267)
BC/BS Adjustments	$	(171,064)
Cigna Adjustments	$	(7,651)
Coventry Adjustments	$	(123,789)
Medicare Adjustments	$	(324,835)
PHS Adjustments	$	(72,798)
PPK Adjustments	$	(97,514)
United Adjustments	$	(83,310)
WPPA Adjustments	$	(8,749)
Non-contractual Adjustments	$	(36,277)
Pre-paid Contract Adj. - PPK	$	(73,886)
Refunds	$	(37,503)
Contractual Adjustments Total:	**$**	**(1,121,820)**

From net sales, the cost of goods sold is subtracted. Cost of goods sold is the cost incurred to create the good or service. This includes direct labor and material. The difference is the gross profit. After this, sales, general, and administrative costs are accounted for. This yields operating income. After any interest expense is accounted for, the pretax income is found. Net income is what remains after taxes and special expenses are paid.

In the case of our medical practice, we subtract our expenses of care provided from the net total revenue. This yields our gross profit for the practice. After this, we account for the costs of our overhead such as general and administrative costs. This number is our operating income. Then, just like with other businesses, we subtract our interest, taxes, and other expenses to yield our net profit or loss for the period of the report.

Bankers and investors like the income statement because they can see where you're making money, spending money, and if you're spending too much or charging too little. They will use the numbers from this report to calculate ratios to determine how healthy your practice really is. We will examine these ratios in Part 3.

Many times, the individual line items are simplified and lumped together to make presenting the data easier and faster to read. However, you should never be afraid to ask questions and request more detail if something doesn't make sense to you. Your accountant usually decides how best to record or classify revenue and expenses. Ask them for their justification or reasoning if you don't understand why they have done it a particular way. This is especially true if they reclassify items. It is an easy way for them to hide money because you will lose the ability to see a trend and variance over time.

Remember, it's your money and your practice. Never be afraid of asking the accountant or manager questions regarding the income statement or any other statement they have had a hand in preparing. Ask lots of questions, especially if you don't understand something on the report. Make certain you know what your accountant is reporting and what they are leaving out and why.

All reports are based upon assumptions or decisions made from the biased perspective of the one who prepared the report. I have known one or two accountants for large practice management firms who were pressured or told to conceal errors the management company made from the practices. Since the physicians didn't know how to read the reports, it was easy for the accountants to hide errors and mistakes from the physicians. They didn't steal money, but they did hide their mistakes that may or may not have cost the physicians' money.

13 | The Revenue Side of Things

Let's start at the top of the report with income. Having income is nice and necessary. However, as I mentioned earlier, it's important to understand when and how you recognized the revenue. Make certain you and your accountant are on the same page when it comes to revenue recognition.

In healthcare, we often bill for services after they have been delivered. There are some cases in which cash payments are received up front for services to be provided (as in a managed care, capitated system, or plastic surgeon's clinic). However, most things are covered or have been approved by the payer before the service is delivered. Many small physician groups recognize their revenue when they receive the cash from the patients and payers. In my practice, I typically don't receive compensation for services rendered until about forty-five days after I submit the bill. Depending on myself and my office staff, the bill may not be submitted for a few days after the patient encounter.

Most payers these days expect a write-off or discount. They typically shoot for a percentage of savings they are looking for. Someone in your office needs to know these contracts inside and out. A summary sheet should be created and updated regularly. This will be important when we discuss budgeting and forecasting later in this book.

The top line is your charges for services provided in that given period. The next line is the adjustments, or contractual write-offs, you've agreed to. It's the amount you're discounting the services against some pre-established fee schedule or chargemaster. This is an important number to watch. If it grows, what happened? Perhaps your payer mix has changed. Why?

In the case of Physicians of America, you'll notice there are two negative numbers in the revenue section of the P&L. The first is for pre-paid cash adjustments for PPK. PPK is an HMO that uses a capitation program. The group received a lump sum of cash at the beginning of the year and must then provide care for the covered lives. These transactions show up on the income statement because cash was received by the business at the beginning of the year. This will also show up on the balance sheet as a liability because POA owes the value of the services. They've already received cash for services to be rendered. They owe their services. Owing anything to anyone is a liability. That's why it appears on the liability side of the balance sheet.

The Expenses Side of Things

The first item after the revenue is the cost of whatever it is we sold to someone. Whether it's goods such as a computer or car, or a service as in a medical consult, the costs of providing that service are listed here. The tricky part is what goes into that figure. It is important that you know and understand what ingredients are baked into this number. It should include all expenses or costs that the company incurred *and* those costs were directly involved in delivering the good or service. Direct costs are those expenses that are directly involved in patient care. They touch the patient in some shape or form. Indirect costs are those costs which do not contribute to the care of the patient. They are more supportive in nature. Examples might be administrative personnel, billing, etc.

Sometimes the decision on what to include or not include is rather easy. It can also be challenging to determine what to put into the costs of services or goods sold. The most fundamental question to ask yourself is, "If I didn't open my doors today, what would I still have to pay for?" If you would still owe rent, then it's not in this number. If you pay employees an hourly wage, then it would be. However, as with anything in life, gray areas abound.

This is a good point to introduce the concept of fixed, variable, and semi-fixed costs. We will dive deeper into these areas in Part 4, but let's look at the topic briefly right now.

Types of Costs

The first type of cost is fixed costs. These are costs that do not change with activity. The company will still have these costs whether their doors are open or not. The cost per unit of fixed cost will go down as activity goes up. Let's assume your medical malpractice is $1,000 each month. It's fixed and doesn't change because you're a very good doctor. The cost per patient will go down as you see more patients. However, the total cost per period won't change if you see 1 or 100 patients in one month.

The second type of cost is variable costs. These costs change as the activity of the company changes. Sell more services, work later and longer, make more widgets, and these costs go up. Do less = spend less. Even though variable costs remain constant per unit, they rise or fall with activity. If it costs you $1 for each lab test your lab draws, the cost of lab draws will depend upon the activity, how many lab draws you did each month. We will discuss fixed and variable costs in greater detail later in the book.

Cost of Goods Sold or Cost of Services

As business owners and leaders, we need to know how much it costs us to provide the good or service to the client or patient. That's what *cost of goods sold* or *cost of services* is. This is how much we paid the people to treat our patients. It's how much we paid for the supplies we used in creating the service. Items that should be included in this number are anything or anyone that was directly involved in the making of the good or service we sold.

Overhead

Overhead will be covered in more detail later, but the concept is simple. Overhead includes any other expense that isn't directly involved in the production of the good or service. It's rent, utilities, janitorial service, and accounting and legal services. These services are necessary for you to operate your clinic but they are not involved in direct patient care.

Depreciation, Again

Depreciation is an important line to notice on an income statement, particularly if your business has lots of tangible assets. It's also a non-cash expense. Cash doesn't actually leave the company. It already did if you paid cash for the asset earlier, or if the expense is a loan payment.

Depreciation is an accounting method for expensing the value of an asset over a given period—typically its useful life. As assets are used, they are worn down and will eventually need to be replaced. Depreciation is the way you account for the expense as you use up the value of the asset.

Let's say you own an ultrasound machine. It probably has a lifespan of three to five years, and it costs $100K. Eventually, the machine will lose its usefulness. Things might break, knobs fall off, and buttons stop working. The connector pins might get bent and no longer work. Someone might spill coffee on it. The point is, depreciation lets you subtract a portion of the value of the asset as an expense. You know you will eventually have to replace it, so you should be saving for a new one. Depreciation is what you should be saving to replace that asset. However, most folks don't do that. They take the expense and run. Poor planning will eventually catch up to them in the end.

This can be a good area for a company to "hide" things. Some might extend the useful life of an asset. In doing so, they reduce this expense and pump up earnings. If this number doesn't seem right, always ask and try to match it to the assets listed on the balance sheet.

The Line

You've probably heard of *the line* when people talk about businesses. In case you're wondering, the line refers to the gross profit. It's what is left over after COGS/COS is removed from the sales revenue.

Most people focus on the information that's above the line. They focus on sales and COGS/COS. However, depending on how things are classified, you might be missing important expenses that are below the line. Always ask questions.

Operating Expenses

Sales and General Administrative Costs

This is where you account for any cost that you didn't account for in COS or operating expenses. It's necessary but doesn't contribute to the creation of the good or service. It's the sales force salaries. It's the office administration's salaries. These people don't touch patients but are necessary for the practice.

Taxes and Other Stuff

Another thing to watch for are one-time expenses. Wall Street uses terms such as write-offs or write-downs. Sometimes they are legit charges such as a restructuring charge during a merger or acquisition or the settlement of a lawsuit. Other times it means they need to correct the books after cooking them, or accounting errors have been discovered.

The Bottom Line

The *bottom-line* means just that—we've accounted for all the cash, paid everyone, and this is what's left over. It's profit, but there are different types of profit.

Gross Profit

Gross profit is an important number to watch. It is also one of the easiest numbers to manipulate because someone—either you or your accountant—gets to decide what goes into COGS or COS and when to recognize revenue. It is critical to communicate with your accountant and understand what exactly is going into your COS number

Consider another scenario with POA. Dr. Charles had been watching the gross profit begin to decline. He examined the revenue side and didn't notice any significant changes in the monthly performance. Revenue appeared to remain stable and steady. But when he looked at the COS, he noticed the number was rising, and seemed to jump from prior months. His horizontal and vertical analysis revealed changes that didn't make sense.

He began to wonder, "Why did our costs to provide our services jump so much all of the sudden?" The most important question he asked was, "What goes into COS?" After a conversation with his accountant, it was revealed the accountant had made a line item change. He re-categorized some overhead salary into COS. This changed the number significantly. Now that Dr. Charles had the information, he could make a clear financial decision. By examining the financial data in its entirety, he was able to notice trends. The lesson here is not just to focus on the numbers but the entire picture.

A friend of my father was a fighter pilot during World War II. He once told a story of how during strafing attacks a pilot could get so focused on the target that they might forget to look at the instruments in the cockpit or the surrounding terrain outside. They got tunnel vision chasing a single target, oblivious to other indicators of their performance. If the pilot focused for too long, they would crash right into the ground because they didn't allow for enough time to pull out of the dive.

We can do the same thing in business. We get so focused on a number or two that we don't take in all of the information the instruments and environment are giving us. Wall Street and Main Street are littered with the remains of businesses, both large and small, that were too focused on just one or two performance numbers.

Operating Profit

Operating profit is our gross profit minus our operating expenses. This includes our sales, general, and administrative costs as well as our amortization and depreciation costs. It is also referred to as EBIT: Earnings Before Interest and Taxes. This number is the profit the business made from actually running the business. We throw out taxes because the tax man really doesn't have anything to do with running our business. The interest expense also has nothing to do with how well you run your business. That's a financing or capital structure decision and has no impact on the day-to-day operations. However, if the interest rate is too high and your monthly interest charge is too much, it might use up all your cash, and you won't be able to meet your daily expenses. We'll discuss the impact of interest and capital structure later.

Net Profit

Net profit, the bottom line, is what matters for most people at the end of the day. Net profit is what is left over after everything else has been subtracted from the revenue. It includes the cost of services, your overhead or operating expenses, the taxes you paid, the interest you paid, and the non-cash expenses such as amortization and depreciation. You will want to watch this number, as it tells you how well you are doing financially. But keep in mind: it is only one piece of the larger puzzle. It's like the oxygen saturation probe we use in the ICU. It tells us some very important data, some of which can be life-threatening. But the readings cannot tell us what is wrong with the patient.

So what if your net profit is declining? There are a few things you should investigate. Start at the top of the P&L and ask questions regarding your revenue. What can you do to increase revenue? Is there room to grow? What's your payer mix like? How can you change that? How do your charges compare in the marketplace? Looking for and implementing methods to increase your revenue can take time. Be prepared for a long process, and be patient.

The second item to look at is the COS. Dig deep into these numbers. What are your costs doing? Rising or staying steady? If they are going up, why and where? How efficient are your processes? What waste or fat can you trim from the system? Again, study your service processes and look for ways to get leaner. Discovering these problems and implementing changes like this takes time. Patience is a virtue—if you have time.

The next item on the list is the overhead or operating expenses. Dig into these numbers and what goes into them. Where might you be able to save money and control costs? Is there any waste you can eliminate in the supporting processes? You might be tempted to make cuts in your supporting services first because their services are not directly tied to the service you provide. Just be careful if you do this and think about the ramifications of your decision. How will the remaining staff think and feel? How might the workload change affect them and their ability to perform well? What might happen to morale not only in the back office but the patient care area as well?

Be careful that you don't get stuck in the trap of trimming expenses. This might be a symptom of a much larger issue. Investigate and discover the real problems behind the declining profits. If you don't address the real problem, you will only postpone the inevitable.

It's best to manage for the long-term. Create a long-term plan to manage your finances. Always look for ways to increase your revenue. It's best to have a plan before you need a plan.

14

When to Recognize Revenue

As we have seen in Chapter 7, there are two accounting methods you can use. While I was working on this book, I consulted with many accountants. One of the issues they regularly mentioned was the question of when to recognize revenue. Since it usually takes folks more than one time around to grasp new information, I think it is necessary to review this concept one more time.

Cash Basis

Cash basis recognizes revenue when cash is received by the company. It does the same with expenses. Cash comes in—revenue is posted. Cash goes out—expenses are posted. This is an easy accounting system to set up and maintain. It's also a lot easier to prepare for tax planning near the end of your fiscal year so you can potentially mitigate or defer taxes.

Let's say you've got $100,000 in cash from revenue, and there are two weeks left in the fiscal year. If you don't drive your expenses up, you'll show a profit of $100,000 and will have a tax bill. However, you could pay off some bills and expenses. You could even pre-pay some accounts to get rid of the cash. In doing this, you'll drive up your expenses, and the bottom line will diminish. If you run into cash flow issues, you can use a line of credit to fund your activities in the short-term. You'll likely save money unless your interest rate on the line of credit is higher than your tax bracket. However, whenever you are taking any actions in contemplation of a tax minimization plan, you should always do so after close consultation with your CPA and/ or your attorney. It's best to spend money to get solid and correct information than to go to jail for tax evasion.

Even though this is an easy system to set up and maintain, it does have some drawbacks, most importantly in matching revenue to expenses. Suppose your days in A/R is about 45–60 days. When using a cash basis accounting system, the cash you receive in March is actually revenue generated from activities in January and February. But on the monthly expense report, you see March's expenses. And the cash you received in January is probably from November. So if January was slow, and expenses were low, but November was busy, then you'll say January is your best month and most productive/ efficient month of the year.

You would be wrong. You would make financial and operational decisions based on a wrong assumption. As we move to bundled payments and leaner healthcare, it will become imperative for you to match your expenses to your revenues. If you don't, you'll be operating with incorrect data and could make wrong decisions.

So what's the best way to match revenues to expenses? By using an accrual basis system.

Accrual Basis

In the system of accounting which is the GAAP standard, you post revenue and expenses when they occur, when the service or good is delivered to the customer. It's a lot more complicated to set up and maintain, but it allows you to easily manage and maintain cost data. In our earlier example, an accrual system would show a bump in revenue and expenses in November. You would be better able to see that more manpower or overtime is required in November than January. An accrual system will help you forecast and budget for seasonality in your services.

15

The Balance Sheet

The balance sheet is for a specific point in time—a snapshot of the financial position of the company. It lists all the assets, liabilities, and equity of the firm at a particular moment in time. It is based on the *accounting equation*: Assets = Liabilities + Stockholder's Equity. Or, said another way, Assets - Liabilities = Stockholder's Equity.

$$\text{Assets} = \text{Liabilities} + \text{Owner's Equity}$$

The major sections of the balance sheet include current assets, investments, PPE (property, plant, and equipment), intangibles, other assets, current liabilities, long-term liabilities, and finally the stockholder's equity. Figure 2.5 is an example of a basic balance sheet. Figure 2.6 is what a real report might look like for you.

Figure 2.5 - Sample Balance Sheet

Balance Sheet for
Specific Point in Time

	Assets			Liabilities	
	Current Assets			**Current Liabilities**	
+	Cash		+	Notes Payable	
+	Cash Equivalents		+	Accounts Payable	
+	Accounts Receivable		+	Interest Payable	
-	Bad Debt Allowance		+	Wages Payable	
+	Inventory		+	Income Taxes Payable	
=	**Total Current Assets**		-	Discount on Notes Payable	
	Long-term Assets		=	**Total Current Liabilities**	
+	Property, Plant, and Equipment			**Long-term Liabilities**	
-	Depreciation		+	Bonds Payable	
+	Intangible Assets		+	Notes Payable	
+	Goodwill, Patents, Copyrights, etc		=	**Total Long-term Liabilities**	
+	Other Assets		=	**Total Liabilities**	
=	**Total Long-term Assets**			Equity	
=	**Total Assets**		+	Paid-In Capital	
			+	Retained Earnings	
			-	Tresuary Stock	
			=	**Total Equity**	
			=	**Total Equity & Liabilities**	

Total Assets = Total Liabilities + Total Equity

Figure 2.6 - Physicians of America Balance Sheet

Balance Sheet
December 31, 2014

Current Assets		Current Liabilities	
Cash in Bank	23,139	Loans Payable-Line Of Credit	44,274
Savings Acct	59,725	Loans Payable-Malpractice	
Patients Receivable	251,944	Loans Payable-Furniture, Furnishings, and Equipment	31,341
Accounts Receivable-Bldg	95,065	FUTA Tax Payable	31
Receipts not Posted	(164)	SUTA Tax Payable	40
Pre-Paid Insurance		**Total Current Liabilities**	**75,686**
Investment Receivables	2,600		
Total Current Assets	**432,309**	*Deferred Revenue*	
		Deferred Accounts Receivable	254,883
Fixed Assets			
Furniture & Fixtures	219,624	**Total Liabilities**	**330,569**
Software	64,093		
Accumulated Depreciation	(266,147)	*Members' Capital*	
Total Property & Equipment	**17,570**	Retained Earnings	53,700
		Members' Capital Accounts	25,470
Other Assets		Members' Curr Yr Capital Contrib.	1,500
Organizational Costs	3,406	General Draws	(430,445)
Accumulated Amortization	(3,406)	Draws-Health, Dental	(14,574)
Utility Deposit	3,215	Draws-Life & Disability Ins.	(6,128)
Inv-TI	5,111	Draws-401(K) Deferral	(38,093)
Total Other Assets	**8,326**	Current Yr Net Income	536,206
		Total Members' Capital	**127,636**
Total Assets	**458,205**		
		Total Liabilities & Capital	**458,205**

The balance sheet is the second important document you will want to look at on a regular basis. It gives you a snapshot of the current balance of your assets, liabilities, and equity. Compare the current balance sheet to past balance sheets to get an idea of whether things are going up or down. Bankers always ask for this document because it tells them how well you're managing your money and assets. They will know how leveraged you are and get an idea of how risky it would be to loan you money.

It Isn't Easy

Understanding the balance sheet isn't as straightforward as the income statement. The income statement makes sense and, for the most, part is logically presented. The income statement shows money coming in minus money going out. Simple. The balance sheet is a different beast. There's a lot of juicy financial information here. It's also where numbers can be fudged easily.

The balance sheet is like a photograph (not one of those new iPhone moving photos, but like an old-fashioned photograph). It's a snapshot of the company's position at a given moment. The income statement covers a period of time. The balance sheet covers a specific point in time. It shows what the company owns and what is owes. The difference between what is owned and owed is your equity. Some months you make lots of money, don't spend too much, and don't borrow money. If that happens, you'll see the equity increase. However, if you have unexpected expenses, borrow money, or sell assets, you'll witness a decline in the equity. The beauty of the balance sheet is that it uses the accounting equation. The danger is in what gets put into which variable of the equation.

Your Net Worth

The balance sheet is what your bank uses when considering whether or not to give you a personal loan for that new home or car. On the application, you put all the assets you own on one side of the sheet, and all the debt you have on the other side. They do this so they can easily total your assets and debts. Then your banker subtracts your debt from your assets. What is left over is your net worth.

In a business, the net worth is the owner's equity. The concept is the same. Both scenarios use the financial equation. For your practice and personal life, knowing what you owe and what you own is powerful and will guide you as you make decisions.

Reading the Report

When you are reading a balance sheet, a few items should always be present in the report. First, since it is a snapshot in time, you should see a particular date listed. It might be the end of the month, the end of the quarter, or the end of the year, but it should be a specific date.

The layout of the report is more of a preference, determined by you or your accountant. Some reports list assets on the left and liabilities and equity on the right. Others prefer to list assets on the top, then liabilities, and then finally equity. It really doesn't matter how the information is presented. Pick whichever method is easiest for you to study and quickly read. Then, practice reading the reports and ask questions about things you don't understand.

16

Assets

An asset is something that possesses value or can be used in the production a good or service. Assets may be tools, machines, knowledge, processes, etc. that work to create future economic benefit for the firm. Assets appearing on a balance sheet may be either tangible (plant, property, land, goods, inventory, work in progress), or intangible (trademarks, patents, copyrights, goodwill). They are also listed regarding their lifespan or the ability to convert them to cash. Many assets lose their ability to produce revenue over time and therefore are depreciated as their value decreases. Assets are typically listed as current assets and long-term assets. Figure 2.7 shows the typical asset seen on a balance sheet.

Figure 2.7 - Asset Classifications

Assets

Current Assets	Long-term Assets
Cash	Land & Buildings
Marketable Securities	Accumulated Depreciation
Government Bonds	Patents
Common Stock	Copyrights
Certificates of Deposit	Goodwill
Accounts Receivable (A/R)	
Inventories	
Prepaid Expenses & Rent	
Supplies	

Current Assets

These are assets which have an operating cycle of one year or less. Stated another way, current assets can be converted into cash in less than one year. These include:

Cash

Marketable Securities

These are financial instruments that can be easily converted into cash. Examples include government bonds, common stock, and certificates of deposit.

Accounts Receivable (A/R)

Accounts receivable represents money that is owed to the company for goods or services that have already been provided or performed by the company.

Inventories

Inventory is the goods on hand that are ready for sale to the customer.

Prepaid Expenses and Rent

Some expenses are paid for in advance and then used up over time.

Long-term Assets

These assets possess an operating cycle of greater than one year. It can be expected that it will take longer than a year to convert these assets into cash. Examples of long-term assets would include:

Land and Buildings

All land and buildings should have a useful lifespan greater than one year, and it can take more than 12 months to convert the land or building into cash.

Machinery

This is equipment that is needed for the production of the good or service.

Accumulated Depreciation

Depreciation is a method of tracking how much of an asset's value or usefulness have been used up over time.

Patents

Patents are the legal rights of the owner or inventor of a product or concept.

Goodwill

In the event of an acquisition of an intangible asset (such as the value of the brand, good customer relationships, etc.), goodwill is used to account for that value.

The Assets: Current Assets

Assets are listed in order of their liquidity with those being most easily converted into cash shown first.

Liquid Assets

Liquid assets can easily and quickly be converted into cash should the need arise. Assets in this class are cash and cash equivalents.

Sometimes you'll see this reported as marketable securities on the balance sheet. Another term used is short-term investments. Assets that fall into this classification are short-term investments that can be sold such as bonds, stocks, and CODs.

Accounts Receivable

Accounts receivable, or A/R, is the amount of money owed to the company for services or goods already provided to the customer. It's what they've promised to pay you. In healthcare or any industry, sometimes we don't get all that we are owed. To account for that, using historical or industry data, we make an allowance for bad debt. We basically say, "We know we aren't going to see a portion of this money. So we'll just write it off ahead of time."

In your clinic, A/R would be the amount of money you are expecting to receive from both the patient and third party payers for rendering your services. It is what you are owed for taking care of the patient. This number must be watched very carefully, especially over time.

Here is an important place where the income statement and balance sheet are linked. The allowance for bad debt is also on the income statement as an expense. Sometimes, people will "fudge" or change this number to affect the profits since a lower bad debt allowance will push up the bottom line. So if you see a decline in the bad debt allowance expense, look at the balance sheet and see what is happening. Always ask, "Does this make sense? What is really happening here to account for these changes? Is the A/R rising or dwindling?" A/R is an example of why you should always look at these financial records together.

Inventory

Service-based companies don't hold inventory in the same way other businesses do. Manufacturers, wholesalers, retailers, and the like hold inventory for resale. The inventory used by service providers is typically used in the production of the service. Needles, bandages, and those comfortable paper gowns are not inventory as much as they are needed for the service provided. They are necessary for the delivery of care and must be managed to ensure you've got them on hand, but they are recorded as supplies on hand and then as expenses rather than assets for resale.

In a manufacturing business, you will see inventories broken down into three classifications: raw materials, work in process (WIP), and finished goods. Each is simply a step further down the road to creating a product. You might see these listed on a balance sheet of a company like Ford or Boeing.

In retail businesses, their inventory is what they have for sale to the customer. Walmart has clothing, pens, and shampoo as their inventory. Apple has computers and iPhones. Eddie Bauer has clothing.

Some clinics will list their supplies in this line item. It will depend upon what you and your accountant agree upon.

The important take-home point is this: if you see inventory listed on a balance sheet for a medical practice, ask why. What goes into that number?

Supplies

In addition to inventory, your business will need supplies to support the activity it performs. These supplies would include needles, bandages, and those really cool paper gowns. How you track them and determine the value of them is up to you—how accurate and complicated you want to get, and how expensive a system you want to create. Watch the balance over time and track the trend. Are you carrying too much in supplies or not enough?

Prepaid Expenses

Prepaid expenses are bills you've paid but have not yet received services for. They are costs that have been paid for but have not yet been used up. Examples are items like rent, insurance premiums, salary advances, utilities, etc. These are assets because you have a claim against someone else's assets, goods, or services. These expenses will be reduced as the benefit of the good or service is received by the company.

The Assets: Long-term Assets

The second classification of assets is long-term assets. Long-term assets are divided into tangible assets, intangible assets, investments, and other (because accountants always want a line item they can dump stuff into).

The Tangible Assets

Property, Plant, and Equipment

Property, plant, and equipment (PPE) is the line item where all of the fixed assets of the company are reported. This includes buildings, machinery (x-ray machines, computers), and any other physical asset owned by the company. The PPE figure is listed as the total cost of the assets. It's whatever the company paid for the assets, and not what today's fair market value might be. Even though the office building and land you bought ten years ago are now worth double what you paid for them, that valuation isn't reflected on the balance sheet. This is the conservatism principle we discussed at the beginning of the book. We know what the cold hard facts are—what you actually paid for the building and land. Anything else is a guess or estimate.

Also remember, if we did report an increase in the value of the building and land, we would need to report the gain as income on the income statement. But that's not real income and gets into fuzzy accounting and math, the likes of which have gotten many a business into trouble.

Machinery

Machinery is equipment used to produce the service or good of the practice. This would include anything we use to treat the patient. Examples would be an ultrasound machine, x-ray machines, therapy tables, etc. Remember, these assets are recorded and reported at their historical cost. They are depreciated over the useful life of the asset and listed as accumulated depreciation.

Accumulated Depreciation

With the exception of land, all assets of the business will wear out. It's just the nature of life. Things wear down, and thus they lose their value. Accumulated depreciation is how you account for the loss of your assets' value. It's how you track and account for the value of the asset you've used up or converted into work that generated income.

It's important to know and understand how each asset type or class is being depreciated. If you see a big bump in the depreciation from prior years, ask why and what method is being used. Since depreciation goes on the income statement as an expense, maybe your accountant is trying to drive down profits and avoid paying taxes. If you don't know, ask questions.

There are several ways to depreciate an asset. The easiest and most straightforward method is the straight-line method.

$$\frac{\text{Cost - Salvage Value}}{\text{Estimated Useful Life}} = \text{Annual Depreciation}$$

In this method, you subtract the salvage value from the cost of the asset and divide by the asset's useful life. Then each year you deduct this amount from the book value of the asset. Book value is the net amount the asset is still worth. So, if your asset cost $100,000 and has a lifespan of 4 years and a salvage value of $20,000, your annual depreciation would be $20,000 per year. After two years, the asset's book value is $60,000.

There are a few other methods of depreciation.

With *sum of the year digits*, each year depreciation is taken at a reduced amount for each year of the life of the asset. It's a form of accelerated depreciation.

Units of activity depreciation reduce the value of the asset based on how much it was used each year. Use the asset a lot in a year, take a larger depreciation expense. Use the asset a little, take a smaller depreciation expense.

Reducing balance depreciation reduces the value of an asset by a fixed percentage each period. The depreciation expense gets smaller with each year as the difference between the book value and residual value of the asset gets smaller.

Leases

Leases are placed into one of two categories: capital or operating leases. If you have any ownership of the leased asset, then it's a capital lease. Otherwise, it's an operating lease. Only capital leases will appear on a balance sheet. Operating leases will appear on the income statement. If you want to clean up your balance sheet, you sell your leveraged assets and then lease assets used in the operations of your business. This is a method that is frequently used to fudge the numbers. Sometimes it a legitimate financial decision to lease, but other times it is a way to hide things.

Investments

Long-term investments are listed here. These can be loans made by the company to individuals and other companies that will be held to maturity. Equity securities are also long-term investments.

Intangible or Other Assets

Intellectual Property

Intellectual property is your know-how. Perhaps you've got some ideas coming out of your R&D that are game-changers or money-makers. It might be your industry-leading processes or systems. Most typically, though, intellectual property is your patents, trademarks, and copyrights.

Patents are the legal rights of the owner or inventor of a product or concept. They are granted by the Federal government and have a lifespan of 20 years. Patents are reported at their acquisition cost and are amortized over the life, or useful life, of the patent.

Trademarks are very distinctive names, images, or words used by a company. Coke is a trademark. Many times slogans are trademarked as well, such as "I'm Lovin' It." Copyrights pertain to pieces of art such as music, artwork, and written work. Copyrights last 70 years beyond the life of the author.

Goodwill

Goodwill is found on the balance sheets of a company that has acquired other companies. It is the difference between what the acquired company is valued at and what they paid for the acquisition. It's brand-name, value-in-the-marketplace kind of stuff—completely intangible in nature. Sometimes, companies will have to write this down as an expense if the acquisition doesn't pan out as planned. For example, if the company is buying ABC, Inc. for $1M, but ABC only has $850K in tangible physical assets, then $150K would be booked as goodwill on the balance sheet. Said another way, you paid $150K more than the tangible assets of the company. That excess has to be accounted for somewhere, so it goes into goodwill.

17

Liabilities

Liabilities are debts owed by the firm to someone else. They are the future sacrifices of economic benefits because of the present obligations of the firm. Like assets, liabilities are also categorized as current and long-term. Figure 2.8 shows a list of common liabilities that will appear on a balance sheet.

Figure 2.8 - Liabilities Classification

Liabilities

Current Liabilities	Long-term Liabilities
Loans and Lines of Credit	Notes Payable
Federal & State Taxes	Long-term Credit Agreements
Retirement Account Payments	Bonds Payable
Deferred Accounts Receivable	Deferred Taxes
	Long-term Leases
	Pensions

Current liabilities are usually due within one year and include:

Loans and Lines of Credit

Small businesses frequently take out loans for the purchase of property and equipment. Many will also secure a line of credit that can be used when the amount of cash on hand is insufficient to meet the outstanding bills. If you have overdraft protection on your checking account, then you have a line of credit.

Federal and State Taxes

What you owe the government in terms of taxes is usually an estimate. The final amount won't be known until the books for that particular period have been closed. You know you will owe money, so you account for it with an estimate on your balance sheet.

Retirement Account Payments

If you have a retirement plan in your business, you probably don't pay into the plan on a regular basis. The common practice is to keep track of the amount of money that is owed to the plan and record it as a liability on the balance sheet. This number is important to follow because it can get quite large and is due at a specific time as mandated by federal law.

Deferred Revenue

Deferred revenue is a liability because it represents money the company has received for goods or services that have not yet been supplied or performed. The company still owes (has to deliver) the goods or services.

Long-term liabilities are due over periods of time longer than one year. These would include:

- Notes payable
- Long-term credit agreements
- Bonds payable
- Deferred taxes
- Long-term leases
- Pensions

It's important to realize that liabilities are a part of life and doing business. Sometimes you must borrow money to make money. Sometimes you would rather pay a little bit in interest to hold onto your cash should you need it in the case of an emergency. We will discuss financial decision-making later in this book as we examine possible capital structure issues.

Current Liabilities

Current liabilities are those debts which are due within one year. There are a few types of current liabilities you might see on a balance sheet.

Current Portion of Long-term Debt

Let's assume you've borrowed $200,000 for a new ultrasound machine. You purchased it on terms, borrowed the money, and each year you must pay $50,000 toward the loan balance. $50,000 would appear in the current liabilities section, and $150,000 would appear in the long-term liabilities section. The following year, since you've paid down $50,000, your current liabilities will show $50,000, but your long-term liabilities will show a balance of $100,000. This pattern will continue until you have paid the balance in full.

Short-term Loans

These are lines of credit (or revolving lines of credit) that you might use if you run into cash flow issues and need to make payroll. They are just like credit cards, and their entire balance due is shown here.

Accounts Payable

Accounts payable, A/P, is what you owe people for stuff you've bought. Perhaps you purchase your medical supplies on terms such as net 60. The vendor has given you 60 days to pay them for the goods or services they have provided. If you don't use cash for things you buy, then it gets put into A/P.

Accrued Expenses

This is the bucket where debts are put if the money wasn't for things directly involved in the business process. Accrued salary, legal fees, accounting fees, interest owed, and the like are dumped into this line item. They appear here because these fees weren't paid or recorded in your accounts payable ledger at the time your financial reports were made. At some later point, your accountant will classify these transactions so that the books are correct. Accrued Expenses is a holding bucket until things can be sorted out.

A big number that might show up on your current liabilities portion of the balance sheet is any accrued pension obligations. Sometimes groups like to postpone funding their employees' retirement plans for as long as they can. This number can grow quickly, and if you haven't budgeted properly, you could wind up running out of cash, hitting your line of credit, and even getting in trouble with the federal government. I would encourage you to watch this number closely and have a plan for dealing with it when the balance is due.

Unearned Income

Unearned income is money that you've received in advance for services or goods yet to be provided. It's the value of the services or goods you owe someone. You'll see this line item frequently if you participate in a capitation health care plan.

Long-term Liabilities

Long-term liabilities are those debts which aren't due within one year. Examples of this are deferred taxes, deferred compensation, mortgages, etc.

Notes Payable

These are loans that mature over a period greater than one year. An example would be a mortgage note which may be anywhere from 10 to 50 years and secured by a piece of real estate.

Bonds Payable

A bond is a debt that you've sold someone in exchange for a specified interest rate over a specific period. Sometimes bonds are convertible to stocks, but it depends on how the debt and contract between you and whoever buys your debt are structured. Small practices likely won't have bonds, but larger hospitals and companies will.

Deferred Taxes

Deferred taxes occur because of the various methods of depreciation and the differences between what a company can deduct for accounting and tax purposes. The accounting that goes into this line item is beyond the scope of this book and the interest of the author. That's why you hire a CPA and tax attorney.

18 | Stockholders' Equity

Stockholders' equity is a broad term that refers to the residual ownership interest in the assets of a company after it has settled all of its liabilities and paid all of its debts. It is how much value the investors would have if they closed up shop, sold everything and paid everybody.

Stockholders' equity has two basic components: capital stock and retained earnings. Capital stock is sometimes referred to as paid-in capital, especially with smaller companies. The company raises this number by selling shares of ownership to investors. The investors can be anyone (owners, employees, outside investors).

There are two ways for the company to increase stockholder equity. First, the shareholders invest money directly into the company. This is usually the case at the beginning of a company. This money is recorded on the balance sheet as paid-in capital.

The second method is from retained earnings. Retained earnings are those earnings the company acquires over time and keeps for itself. This number comes from the income statement as net income. Sometimes companies will use some of the income to pay dividends. If they don't pay out all of the income as a dividend, then it is recorded on the balance sheet as retained earnings. Apple is an example of a company with huge retained earnings. Up until a few years ago, Apple had just been dumping profits or retained earnings into cash.

Depending on the company, stockholders' equity may have other accounts such as benefit plans and retirement allocations.

19 | How Assets, Liabilities, and Equity Affect Each Other

Purchase of Equipment

Let's say Physicians of America has $200,000 in cash and $50,000 in A/R and $25,000 in A/P. They want to buy an ultrasound machine, but it costs $200,000. That would take all of their cash. However, the manufacturer has offered them a line of credit and will let them purchase it on terms. Let's look at their balance sheet before the purchase in Figure 2.9.

Figure 2.9 - Balance Before Purchase of Equipment

Assets			Liabilities		
Cash	$	200,000	A/P	$	25,000
A/R	$	50,000			
PPE	$	-	Total Liabilities	$	25,000
			Equity		
			Stockholder Equity	$	225,000
			Retained Earnings		
			Total Equity	$	225,000
Total	$	250,000	Total Liab & Equity	$	250,000

Here we see that there is $225,000 in owner's equity. The assets and liabilities and equity side balance. Now let's see what happens when they purchase the new ultrasound machine in Figure 2.10.

Figure 2.10 - Balance Sheet After Purchase of Equipment

Assets			Liabilities	
Cash	$	200,000	A/P	$ 25,000
A/R	$	50,000	Ultrasound Loan	$ 200,000
PPE	$	200,000	Total Liabilities	$ 225,000
			Equity	
			Stockholder Equity	$ 225,000
			Retained Earnings	
			Total Equity	$ 225,000
Total	$	450,000	Total Liab & Equity	$ 450,000

You'll notice that the equity hasn't changed. The group gained an asset, and it was offset or balanced by the corresponding liability. What happens if they put some cash down? We see the results in Figure 2.11

Figure 2.11 - Balance Sheet After Purchase with Loan

Assets			Liabilities	
Cash	$	175,000	A/P	$ 25,000
A/R	$	50,000	Ultrasound Loan	$ 175,000
PPE	$	200,000	Total Liabilities	$ 200,000
			Equity	
			Stockholder Equity	$ 225,000
			Retained Earnings	
			Total Equity	$ 225,000
Total	$	425,000	Total Liab & Equity	$ 425,000

We see that cash decreases by $25,000, and so does the amount of the loan they take out to buy the machine, $175,000. The value of the asset remains the same because it cost $200,000. You'll notice the assets of the company have decreased by $25,000. This is because we transferred the value from cash to the new machine. Likewise, liabilities have decreased as well. But the important thing to realize is that the owner's equity has remained unchanged throughout all of these transactions.

20 | You Can Make Money and Go Broke

Cash Really is King

Cash is all that matters at the end of the day. Without it, the business dries up and folds. Cash is needed to pay employees, lenders, suppliers, and overhead expenses. Cash is needed for maintenance of assets.

Just like the circulatory system of the human body, cash flows through a company, a source of energy to get work done. The only statement that will give you a clear picture of this flow of cash is the cash flow statement. You can have sales or revenue and still go bankrupt if you don't know where your cash is coming from or going to.

Profitability vs. Going Broke

It is quite possible to have a profitable company yet go bankrupt. Consider the income statement and cash flow statement below as an example.

Figure 2.12 - Cash Flow Analysis Scenario 1

	Jan	Feb	Mar	Apr	May	Jun	Jul
Charges	$ 25,000	$ 25,000	$ 25,000	$ 25,000	$ 25,000	$ 25,000	$ 25,000
COS	$ 15,000	$ 15,000	$ 15,000	$ 15,000	$ 15,000	$ 15,000	$ 15,000
Gross Profit	$ 10,000	$ 10,000	$ 10,000	$ 10,000	$ 10,000	$ 10,000	$ 10,000
Expenses	$ 7,500	$ 7,500	$ 7,500	$ 7,500	$ 7,500	$ 7,500	$ 7,500
Net Profit	$ 2,500	$ 2,500	$ 2,500	$ 2,500	$ 2,500	$ 2,500	$ 2,500
Cash Flow							
Beginning Cash	$ 10,000	$ (12,500)	$ (10,000)	$ (7,500)	$ (5,000)	$ (2,500)	-
Operations							
Cash from Charges	$ -	$ 25,000	$ 25,000	$ 25,000	$ 25,000	$ 25,000	$ 25,000
Cash to Employees	$ 15,000	$ 15,000	$ 15,000	$ 15,000	$ 15,000	$ 15,000	$ 15,000
Cash to Expenses	$ 7,500	$ 7,500	$ 7,500	$ 7,500	$ 7,500	$ 7,500	$ 7,500
Net Cash Flow	$ (12,500)	$ (10,000)	$ (7,500)	$ (5,000)	$ (2,500)	-	$ 2,500

Dr. Harris starts a clinic with $10,000 in the bank. She thought it would be enough to get things going. However, not all payers pay promptly in healthcare. But her employees want to be paid on time. The phone company and electric company want to be paid on time as well. She pays all of her bills on time while waiting for the cash from the payers to arrive.

According to her income statement, she's making money. If that's the case, why is she running out of money? The cash flow statement shows the cause for concern.

Fortunately for Dr. Harris, her payers like her a lot and pay her within thirty days as in the example above. It will only take seven months until she begins to build up a cash reserve for her clinic. But what happens if her days in A/R is sixty days? It gets uglier. In fact, it will take a full twelve months before she has any cash in the bank to pay her bills. She will have to spend the first year of operating the clinic living on a line of credit, borrowing money from friends and family, or selling equity to investors to raise cash. We can see what happens in Figure 2.13 as a result of these new assumptions.

Figure 2.13 – Cash Flows for Scenario 2

	Jan	Feb	Mar	Apr	May	Jun	Jul	Aug	Sep	Oct	Nov	Dec	Jan
Charges	$ 25,000	$ 25,000	$ 25,000	$ 25,000	$ 25,000	$ 25,000	$ 25,000	$ 25,000	$ 25,000	$ 25,000	$ 25,000	$ 25,000	$ 25,000
COS	$ 15,000	$ 15,000	$ 15,000	$ 15,000	$ 15,000	$ 15,000	$ 15,000	$ 15,000	$ 15,000	$ 15,000	$ 15,000	$ 15,000	$ 15,000
Gross Profit	$ 10,000	$ 10,000	$ 10,000	$ 10,000	$ 10,000	$ 10,000	$ 10,000	$ 10,000	$ 10,000	$ 10,000	$ 10,000	$ 10,000	$ 10,000
Expenses	$ 7,500	$ 7,500	$ 7,500	$ 7,500	$ 7,500	$ 7,500	$ 7,500	$ 7,500	$ 7,500	$ 7,500	$ 7,500	$ 7,500	$ 7,500
Net Profit	$ 2,500	$ 2,500	$ 2,500	$ 2,500	$ 2,500	$ 2,500	$ 2,500	$ 2,500	$ 2,500	$ 2,500	$ 2,500	$ 2,500	$ 2,500
Cash Flow													
Beginning Cash	$ 10,000	$ (12,500)	$ (35,000)	$ (32,500)	$ (30,000)	$ (27,500)	$ (25,000)	$ (22,500)	$ (20,000)	$ (17,500)	$ (15,000)	$ (12,500)	$ (10,000)
Operations													
Cash from Charges	$ -	$ -	$ 25,000	$ 25,000	$ 25,000	$ 25,000	$ 25,000	$ 25,000	$ 25,000	$ 25,000	$ 25,000	$ 25,000	$ 25,000
Cash to Employees	$ 15,000	$ 15,000	$ 15,000	$ 15,000	$ 15,000	$ 15,000	$ 15,000	$ 15,000	$ 15,000	$ 15,000	$ 15,000	$ 15,000	$ 15,000
Cash to Expenses	$ 7,500	$ 7,500	$ 7,500	$ 7,500	$ 7,500	$ 7,500	$ 7,500	$ 7,500	$ 7,500	$ 7,500	$ 7,500	$ 7,500	$ 7,500
Net Cash Flow	$ (22,500)	$ (22,500)	$ 2,500	$ 2,500	$ 2,500	$ 2,500	$ 2,500	$ 2,500	$ 2,500	$ 2,500	$ 2,500	$ 2,500	$ 2,500

Even though Dr. Harris has a profitable clinic, she can still go bankrupt. This is the primary reason most startups fail—they run out of cash. This is why the cash flow statement is critical to have and understand.

Different Sources of Cash

Cash can come from a variety of sources. It can come from sales or charge revenue. It can come from loans and liabilities. Cash can come from investors or owners as additional paid-in capital. Having cash is important, but knowing where the cash comes from is just as critical. The last two sources of cash don't show up on the income statement, just the balance sheet. That's why you always need to review both statements together on a regular basis. One way to see how your cash is flowing is to create a cash flow statement, or a statement of cash flows.

21 | Statement of Cash Flows

The cash flow statement is built from the other two statements. It reports activities for the same period as the income statement. It typically consists of three sections: cash from operating activities, cash from investing activities, and cash from financing activities. It is very difficult to hide things on the statement of cash flows. The cash flow statement allows the firm to see how much cash is being generated from its various activities and more importantly if the firm made a profit for the time period.

If you use QuickBooks, you might notice that this report is one of the options under the reports menu. This report can also be created by hand if your accountant or accounting software doesn't have the ability to generate this report. It takes a little thought to make this report, as it involves pulling numbers from the other two reports. However, it might be more important than the others. The cash flow report will reveal the financial decisions of the company. How did it make its money? Where did it go? How much is left over? Some accountants might not want to make this report if you ask for it. If yours doesn't, get another accountant.

Types of Cash Flow on the Report

Operating Activities

Cash listed under this heading is all the cash that came into and left the company because of the work the company did. If a payer cut you a check, then that money is *from operations* or *provided by operations*. When you pay an employee, it's *cash used by operations* or *cash to operations*. If cash was spent to keep the doors open, it's listed here.

You likely have a healthy company when it can provide enough cash to finance itself without borrowing money or selling equity.

Investing Activities

Investing activities are those in which the company invests cash into things for the benefit of the company. This is typically the acquisition of assets. If the company buys an ultrasound machine, it's listed under *to investing* or *used in investing*. If you sell that old ultrasound machine, it would be *cash from investing*.

This is a good place to see how much investing your company is doing. You may or may not have a lot of investment in your practice. It depends on the services you offer and what you need to provide those services.

Financing Activities

Financing typically refers to borrowing money or paying back debts. You'll see shareholder activities here as well. So, if you borrow money, your cash will go up. You sell stock and get cash, cash goes up. When you pay back the loan or buy back the stock, the cash will go down.

This is an important part to watch closely. How much are you relying on outsiders, from bankers to investors, to finance your business?

22 | A Quick Method to Make Your Own Cash Flow Statement

The cash flow statement is created with data provided by the income statement and balance sheet. If you don't have a cash flow statement provided by your accountant, or you're evaluating another company's financials (say, as an investor), then you can make your cash flow statement with an income statement and two balance sheets, current and past.

Some Important Rules

If an asset increases—cash decreases. So cash is subtracted. If a liability increases—cash increases. So cash is added.

Depreciation is a non-cash expense on the income statement, so we have to add it back into cash.

The cash flow statement has three sections: operating activities, investing activities, and financing activities. A summary of the different types of activities is shown in Figure 2.14

Figure 2.14 - Cash Flow Statement Activity Types

Assets	Activity Types
Cash	Cash
Accounts Receivable (A/R)	Operating
Bad Debt	Operating
Inventories	Operating
Other Notes Receivable	Investing
Plant and Equipment	Investing
Accumulated Depreciation	Operating
Noncurrent Assets	Investing
Liabilities	
Accounts Payable (A/P)	Operating
Salaries Payable	Operating
Short-term Loans Payable	Operating
Other Current Liabiliteis	Financing
Long-term Debt	Financing
Due to Shareholders	Financing
Paid-in Capital	Financing
Retained Earnings	Operating

Creating Your Cash Flow Statement

Creating a cash flow statement isn't difficult, it just requires a little time and knowledge. First, we start with the net income and make adjustments based upon the operating activities. We increase cash from revenues and decrease cash from expenses. The way you adjust the net income might seem counterintuitive, but it does make sense.

For example, we add our depreciation back into the net income because it was deducted on the income statement. It was really a non-cash expense that must be added back into the numbers. Another example would be cash we gained from the sale of an asset. That transaction wasn't an operating activity, so we much subtract that cash from the net income because we want to identify where our cash is coming from. I've created a table in Figure 2.15 to help you as you make your own cash flow statements.

Figure 2.15 – Cash Flow Adjustments by Operating Activities

Adjustments to Net Income
by Operating Activities

+	Depreciation
-	Gain on Sale of Equipment
+	Loss on Sale of Equipment
+	Decrease in Accounts Receivable
-	Increase in Accounts Receivable
+	Decrease in Inventory
-	Increase in Inventory
-	Decrease in Accounts Payable
+	Increase in Accounts Payable
-	Decrease in Accured Expenses
+	Increase in Accured Expenses
+	Decrease in Prepaid Expenses
-	Increase in Prepaid Expenses
-	Decrease in Taxes Payable
+	Increase in Taxes Payable

The next section concerns cash flows from investing activities. Cash flow in this section comes from buying or selling an asset, typically a long-term (noncurrent) asset. It could be the acquisition of a new piece of equipment, a new building, or any other long-term asset. We add the proceeds from the sale of assets and subtract the purchases of property and equipment. Figure 2.16 shows the adjustments made by investing activities.

Figure 2.16 - Cash Flow Adjustments by Investing Activities

Adjustments to Net Income
by Investing Activities

+	Proceeds from Sale of Assets
-	Purchases of Property and Equipment

The final section is the financing activity cash flows. Adjustments made as the result of financing activities is shown in Figure 2.17. Financing activity is when we borrow or pay money back, issue stock, or pay dividends. If we get cash from taking out loans, then we add that cash. If we pay off a debt, we subtract that cash. Basically, if cash comes in from owners' contributions or loans, it gets added in. If it goes out to owners or lenders, it gets subtracted.

Figure 2.17 - Cash Flow Adjustments by Financing Activities

Adjustments to Net Income by Financing Activities

+	Net Borrowing
-	Loan Repayment
-	Principle Payments on Capital Leases
-	Dividends, Distributions, Withdrawals
+	Proceeds from Stock Issuance
+	Owner/Partner Capital Contributions

A Real, Honest-to-goodness Life Example

Let's construct a cash flow statement for POA. We will take information from two balance sheets and begin with the net income from the income statement for 2015. These reports are shown in Figures 2.18-20.

Figure 2.18 - Physicians of America Income Statement 2015

Income Statement

		12/31/15
Gross Charges		
Professional Service Charges	$	1,275,745
Orthopedic Charges	$	8,143
Injection Charges	$	105,328
Immunization Charges	$	104,298
Procedure Charges	$	115,725
Laboratory Charges	$	711,383
Radiology Charges	$	125,539
Hospital Charges	$	124,821
Nursing Home Charges	$	46,825
Miscellaneous Charges	$	2,364
Gross Charges Total	$	2,620,171
Contractual Adjustments	$	(1,066,797)
Net Medical Charges	$	1,553,374
Capitation Revenue	$	138,231
Other Operating Income	$	43,901
Adj to Cash Collections	$	160,886
Total Net Revenue	$	1,896,391
Expenses		
Total Personnel Expense	$	731,954
Total Computer Expense	$	15,128
Total Radiology Expense	$	28,214
Total Laboratory Exp	$	91,885
Total Building Exp	$	235,926
Total Supplies Expense	$	110,688
Total Operating Expenses	$	1,213,795
Total Furn / Equip Exp	$	9,805
Total Purchased Svcs	$	21,785
Total EE Related Svcs	$	25,963
Total Gen & Adm Exp	$	41,886
Non-Op Rev/Exp	$	44,702
Total Overhead	$	144,141
Total Expenses	$	1,357,936
Net Profit	$	538,455

Figure 2.19 - Physicians of America Balance Sheets 2014 and 2015

Balance Sheet
December 31, 2014

Current Assets

Cash in Bank	$	23,139
Savings Acct	$	59,725
Patients Receivable	$	251,944
Accounts Receivable-Bldg	$	95,065
Receipts not Posted	$	(164)
Pre-paid Insurance		
Investment Receivables	$	2,600
Total Current Assets	$	432,309

Fixed Assets

Furniture & Fixtures	$	219,624
Software	$	64,093
Accumulated Depreciation	$	(266,147)
Total Property & Equipment	$	17,570

Other Assets

Organizational Costs	$	3,406
Accumulated Amortization	$	(3,406)
Utility Deposit	$	3,215
Inv-TI	$	5,111
Total Other Assets	$	8,326
Total Assets	$	458,205

Current Liabilities

Loans Payable—Line of Credit	$	44,274
Loans Payable—Malpractice		
Loans Payable—Furniture, Furnishings, and Equipment	$	31,341
FUTA Tax Payable	$	31
SUTA Tax Payable	$	40
Total Current Liabilities	$	75,686

Deferred Revenue

Deferred Accounts Receivable	$	254,883
Total Liabilities	$	330,569

Members' Capital

Retained Earnings	$	53,700
Members' Capital Accounts	$	25,470
Members' Curr Yr Capital Contrib.	$	1,500
General Draws	$	(430,445)
Draws—Health, Dental	$	(14,574)
Draws—Life & Disability Ins.	$	(6,128)
Draws—401(K) Deferral	$	(38,093)
Current Yr Net Income	$	536,206
Total Members' Capital	$	127,636
Total Liabilities & Capital	$	458,205

Balance Sheet
December 31, 2015

Current Assets		
Cash in Bank	$	28,602
Savings Acct	$	61,792
Patients Receivable	$	284,160
Accounts Receivable-Bldg	$	95,065
Receipts not Posted	$	(164)
Pre-paid Insurance		
Investment Receivables	$	1,200
Total Current Assets	$	470,655
Fixed Assets		
Furniture & Fixtures	$	219,624
Software	$	64,093
Accumulated Depreciation	$	(280,246)
Total Property & Equipment	$	3,471
Other Assets		
Organizational Costs	$	3,406
Accumulated Amortization	$	(3,406)
Utility Deposit	$	3,215
Inv-TI	$	3,444
Total Other Assets	$	6,659
Total Assets	$	480,786
Current Liabilities		
Loans Payable—Line of Credit	$	113,702
Loans Payable—Malpractice		
Loans Payable—Furniture, Furnishings, and Equipment	$	14,714
FUTA Tax Payable	$	32
SUTA Tax Payable	$	39
Total Current Liabilities	$	128,487
Deferred Revenue		
Deferred Accounts Receivable	$	253,635
Total Liabilities	$	382,122
Members' Capital		
Retained Earnings	$	50,557
Members' Capital Accounts	$	57,660
Members' Curr Yr Capital Contrib.	$	3,613
General Draws	$	(519,886)
Draws—Health, Dental	$	(9,340)
Draws—Life & Disability Ins.	$	(3,103)
Draws—401(K) Deferral	$	(19,292)
Current Yr Net Income	$	538,455
Total Members' Capital	$	98,664
Total Liabilities & Capital	$	480,786

Figure 2.20 - Physicians of America Cash Flow Statement 2015

Cash Flow Statement
For year ending Dec 31, 2015

Operating Activiites

Net Profit	$	538,455
Change in A/R	$	(32,216)
Net Cash from Operations	$	506,238

Investing Activities

Investment Receivables	$	1,400
Net Cash from Investing	$	1,400

Financing Activities

Net Borrowing	$	69,428
Repayment of Loans	$	(16,627)
Distributions	$	(89,441)
Paid-In Capital	$	32,190
Draws—Insurance	$	8,259
Draws—401k	$	18,801
Med Malpractice Loan	$	(16,122)
Net Cash from Financing	$	6,488

Change in Cash	$	1,055
Beginning Cash	$	82,864
Ending Cash Balance	$	83,919

We look at the changes in the line items of the balances sheets from the year-end of 2014 and 2015. These changes are what we will use to create the cash flow statement.

The first section we build is cash from operating activities—seeing and taking care of patients. We see from the income statement that their net income for 2015 was $538,455. Not too bad for the year. On their income statement, they don't list a depreciation expense. Remember our discussion of cash basis accounting? That's why. It'll become apparent later why they don't list or really need this deduction. If they had listed depreciation, then we would add the non-cash expense back into the net income because cash never left the company.

We also see that their A/R grew by $32,216. That's money they are owed. They delivered services but never received the income. So, we deduct the change in A/R. After throwing in their changes in investing revenue, we have a net cash from operations of $506,238.

The second section to build is the investing section. They didn't purchase any new equipment or assets in 2015, so this area is pretty bare. All they have is $1,400 from an investment they've made in the past.

The last section is financing activities. Here we see a lot of activity. After comparing two balance sheets, we see they borrowed about $69,428 over the course of 2015. They also paid back $16,627 in loans as well as $16,122 in a medical malpractice loan. They also had a number of draws on the equity accounts for insurance, 401K contributions, and general owner draws. They took about $519,866 out of their equity accounts and paid themselves.

After we total each section up, we total all three sections to arrive at the net cash change for 2015. Their cash position changed by $1,055 for 2015. This isn't surprising as this is a small group and they are using a cash basis accounting system. They made all of their money seeing patients and then gave it to themselves. There's nothing wrong with that. However, they might want to watch their borrowing.

The cost-benefit analysis will help you determine the best way to use your cash. Should POA have spent $70,000 on something else rather than using it as an owner distribution? Difficult to say. If they had, each owner would see a reduction in their income by about $23,000. That's a pretty big chunk of cash to take out of your paycheck, especially if you live paycheck to paycheck or have become accustomed to a certain lifestyle. The way you run your business is likely the way you run your personal life.

The important issue is knowing where your cash is coming from and where it is going. The balance sheet and income statement help identify some of the areas, but only the cash flow statement will give you a clear picture of where your cash is headed. If your accountant won't prepare one of the reports for you, then get another accountant. In the meantime, you now know how to make one yourself.

What's Your Cash Position?

There are several items to examine if your cash position isn't good. First, look at the A/R. How quickly are your payers paying? Have you allowed terms that are too lenient? Which payers are paying outside of their contracted terms? How quickly are you submitting your claims? How accurate are your claims when they are submitted? How can the process be improved?

Expenses are another area to examine. How quickly are you paying your vendors? Do you take as much time as your agreements with your vendors allow? Are you carrying too much in supplies or inventory? How long can you wait before you need to reorder? Can you wait a little longer?

There's Power in Knowledge

Understanding how to read and construct a cash flow statement will help you understand how healthy your company is. Where is your cash coming from? From operations—good. From borrowing—maybe not so good. It depends on what you're going to do with that cash. Are you investing enough cash into the company? Which is larger, your investment into new assets or the depreciation of existing assets? Basically, what are you doing with your cash: investing, paying debt, or giving a distribution? That will tell you what you value.

23 | How the Income Statement Affects the Balance Sheet

Now that we've looked at both the income statement and balance sheet separately, let's examine how these two reports are intertwined with each other. Highlight or underline the next statement because it's important. A change on one of these statements almost always has an impact on the other.

This occurs because of the double-entry accounting system your accountant uses. This was mentioned briefly in Part 1 and is key for understanding how the accounts on the various reports affect one another. For example, when Walmart sells an item, inventory is decreased on the balance sheet, and revenue on the income statement is increased. In healthcare, we would see an increase in revenue and a decrease in supplies if they are listed. If we borrow money to pay for operating expenses, then we would see the cost of services increase with an increase in the liabilities on the balance sheet.

Revenue on the income statement will affect cash and A/R on the balance sheet. Cost of services will affect payables. Operating expenses will affect prepaid expenses and payables. Net income affects owner's equity as retained earnings.

Let's consider Physicians of America again as an example. Let's say that at the end of the year there is a net income of $100,000. That's the bottom line number on the income statement. On the balance sheet, it will be shown as retained earnings unless they distribute the cash to the owners. If that's the case, then it would appear as a distribution on the equity side of the balance sheet. Either way, once something changes on the income statement or balance sheet, a change should be reflected on the other report.

24 | Your Most Valuable Asset That Doesn't Appear on the Balance Sheet

The Value of Employees

Service industries, like healthcare, are run by people. The services we provide are created by our people: our employees. They hold the knowledge and skills the company needs to provide the service they offer. The real value of the employee lies in their skillsets and knowledge. But where do they appear on the balance sheet? The answer is, they don't. Instead, employees appear on the expense report as an expense—the cost of doing business. Many times managers or leaders tend to view employees as expenses, something to be cut or controlled. They tend to forget that the people they manage and lead are critical to the success of the company. It is the group as whole that provides the services which generate the revenue the company needs.

Good companies will invest in their employees, take care of them, and help them grow and improve. The belief is that the investment in the employee will offer a return to the company. There are numerous examples of companies that view employees as assets rather than expenses. Southwest Airlines, Chick-fil-A, and Koch Industries are just a few names that come to mind.

Other companies take the opposite viewpoint. They view employees as costs needing to be curtailed. They believe there is an endless supply of talent and they can replace anyone at any time and be okay. My suggestion to you is to view employees as assets, not expenses. Better yet, view them as the people they are. Once you do that, you will realize that they are your greatest assets.

PART THREE

How Healthy Is Your Practice?

25 | You Can Only Fix What You Know Is Broken

Dr. Nicole Griffiths loved being a doctor and seeing patients. It was all she wanted to do since she was a child. But lately, she had been distracted by the mood of the office staff. People seemed on edge. Stress was in the air, and she didn't understand why. Now her day was about to begin, and she had to focus on her patients. She took a sip of her coffee. *I'll ask Cathy about this later.* She put down the cup, grabbed her stethoscope, and headed down the hall to the last door on the right.

She knocked and entered the room with a smile on her face. "Good morning, Mary. How are you today?" she asked with a big grin.

"I'm doing well, Doctor. Did you have a good weekend?" Mary asked.

"Yes, I did. How about you?"

"It was good. Got out in the yard and did some work with Charles. We definitely got our exercise cleaning up the place. My sugars were a bit off, though. Thought I would reward myself for all that hard work. Guess I shouldn't have done that," Mary replied.

Nicole sat down on her stool, placed the chart on the countertop, and smiled. "That's perfectly OK. Working outside with someone is good for you in many different ways. I'm glad to hear you're doing it. Speaking of your diabetes, how have your sugars been lately? May I see your logs?"

Mary squirmed a little in her seat. She glanced down at the floor, paused for a second, and then began to fumble through her purse. "Let's see…it's in here somewhere. I'm sorry, Dr. Griffiths, but I might not have been really good at keeping my journal up to date." She pulled out a small notebook and handed it to her. "I probably should start a new journal, one that's not as mangled as that."

Nicole took the book from Mary and began to flip through the pages until she reached the last page of entries. "You're missing some days here, but the overall trend seems good. It would appear you're doing well with your blood sugar. We'll wait for your A1C test results before I make any changes, though."

"About that—why do I have to get blood drawn each time I come here? They usually poke me a few times before they get blood. Why are they drawing my blood all the time?" Mary asked.

"Well, we do that so we can see how well the therapies are working. I won't know if I need to make a change in your diabetes medication or your diuretics if I don't have lab values. I know it's not fun, but without it, I'm not as a good of a doctor as I can be."

Mary shrugged her shoulders. "I suppose if you need it, you need it."

They finished their conversation with Nicole explaining that she was going to make a few changes and then see how those would do over the next few months. She thanked Mary for coming in and moved on to the next patient. As the end of the day approached, she began to feel tired. She wasn't tired because of the day's work, but because of what the evening might bring. She would have to sit through another partner meeting and discuss the practice. She found it boring and mindless at times.

After her last patient left for the day, Nicole headed down the hall to the meeting room. Approaching her from the other direction was Dr. Bill Clark. He was a senior partner and had been with the practice for decades. She liked him but often thought he was crazy. He enjoyed these meetings a little too much.

"Good evening, Nicole. How are you?" Bill asked with a smile.

"Hi, Bill. I'm fine. Just looking forward to yet another meeting. I don't really see why we need to meet so frequently and pore over the same reports each time."

Bill nodded. "Yes, it can be tedious at times, but it's very important for us to do this on a regular basis. Otherwise, how will we know how the practice is doing financially? If we don't monitor these reports regularly, how will we know when we are in trouble or what changes we should make? It's important for the future of the practice that we do this. It's no different than when we treat our patients. Why do you check A1Cs or electrolytes over time? The same principles apply to both treating patients and running a business."

Nicole thought of her very first conversation with Mary that morning. Perhaps, she should think of the practice as a patient and do what she could to keep it healthy and vibrant. As she sat down at the table, Nicole had a different mindset toward the meetings.

26 | Have a Plan

No matter what you're doing in life, you should have a plan. Set valid objectives and activity goals. In medical school, we are taught how to write SOAP notes. Subjective, Objective, Assessment, and *Plan*. Our job is to create a treatment plan for the patient. Yet, sometimes we don't have a plan to grow or maintain our practice. We tend to "wing it" and skate by or get lucky. As our economy gets leaner and leaner and the focus of payers and patients shifts toward the costs of healthcare, you must have a plan.

Plans aren't hard to make. The process is actually quite easy. The simpler the plan, the easier it is to implement, and some of the most successful plans are the simple ones. So it's not the plan that is hard. What is difficult is investing the time and energy to make a plan, and that is what most people fail to do: they don't invest in a plan for their practice. If it's easy to do, it's easy not to do. I've found Laurence Peter of the Peter Principle to be accurate when he says that if you don't know where you're going (you don't have a plan), you'll always end up somewhere, but it'll likely be where someone else wants you to be.

If you want to succeed in the business of healthcare, take a SOAP note approach to your business and make a plan.

SOAP Notes

I remember the first day of my clinical rotations. The first thing we were taught is how to write a SOAP note. I'm sure you remember that too: subjective, objective, assessment, plan. It's a standard that is universal across the medical field. It's how we think and communicate with one another. We use this tool to organize our thoughts as we determine the best course of action to solve the problem. If we take a similar approach to running our practices, we might find managing our finances easier.

What's the first rule of a SOAP note? It's to be written every time we see the patient. Whether that's daily, every other day, monthly, etc., we make a record of the visit. We should be examining our practice's finances on a regular basis as well. As we examine the financial reports, using the same method, we can easily get a picture of the financial status and develop a game plan for improvement.

The first part of a SOAP note is the *subjective* portion. How does the patient feel? What are their symptoms? What is going on? In our case, we might ask, "How are we performing this week or this month? What's our revenue for this period? How do our operations look and feel? Did it feel like we were busy or slow? What are our people saying?" Then write down what you think the answers are.

The *objective* section comes next. In it, we might write down the real metrics we are following that help provide answers to our questions. We might look at visits per day or total visits for the period. We might also look back at a previous period for comparison and trend-spotting.

Assessment is where we pool all the data together and develop a picture of what's going on—how are we doing financially? What direction are we trending? What are the ratios telling us? How do we compare to industry benchmarks? Are we getting better, treading water, or sinking?

The plan is where we formulate our actions plans. What decisions and actions do we need to make today so that we reach our goals and objectives tomorrow? What do the financial reports suggest that we do if we are to be profitable tomorrow?

Whether you think so or not, you've got the skills to make good financial decisions. You simply must learn a little more information. That's what this book is for.

27

The Financial Analysis Process

There are three basic strategies in financial analysis reporting. Two are snapshots of today (ratios and vertical analysis), and the third looks at what happened over a period of time (horizontal analysis).

Ratios

Ratios provide information on the relationship between various line items on the income statement and balance sheet. They can give insight into the profitability, solvency, liquidity, and operational management of the organization. They are like our ankle-brachial index or the HDL to LDL ratio. They compare two pieces of information from a report to give you an idea of what is going on.

Vertical Analysis

Vertical analysis allows you to see how the items on the P&L not only add up to the bottom line but also the percentage of their contribution. How much of your operating cost is in supplies? What percentage of your total costs are personnel costs? Where is your revenue coming from? What service lines are doing the best? What is trending up and down? Does it make sense? Who is your biggest payer? Who is your best payer? Are they the same?

Horizontal Analysis

Horizontal analysis compares the financial reporting and statements from one time period to another. It lets you spot and track trends and see if your decisions produce the desired effect. This is like tracking a patient's A1C over time. It's a great way to see if you're reaching your financial goals.

28 | The Financial Ratios

Ratios are Everywhere

If you stop and think about it, we have ratios for most things in life. Whether it's how many miles per gallon we get in our car to how much we spend per hour on electricity, we deal with ratios every day. Sports enthusiasts love ratios. They can talk all day about a player or team's stats. RBI, the percent of free throws made…they know the statistics. Why? Because they use this information to compare one player to another player and one team to another team. Las Vegas uses ratios and analysis all the time; that's how they come up with the odds ratios.

Bankers, lenders, and investors will use ratios to determine how healthy your company is. They will compare you to industry standards to determine your risk, which in part is based on how well you manage your business. This is only one reason why financial intelligence is critical. The most important reason is so that you can understand and manage your business or clinic.

Financial ratios are an important tool for any manager or individual responsible for operating a small business or business unit. Ratios allow them to quickly see how healthy the firm is financially and to track performance over time. By understanding where the ratios come from and what they indicate, a small business owner is better equipped to make strategic financial decisions.

The ratios discussed here will involve liquidity (risk to investors), utilization (how efficiently the firm makes money), profitability, and financial strength ratios. Each is important, but the reader is encouraged to pick a few that make the most sense to them and use these regularly.

29

Liquidity Ratios

In financial terms, liquidity refers to the firm's ability to convert their assets to cash in a short time, usually less than one year. This is important when considering the liabilities of the firm in conjunction with the income statement and revenue projections. These ratios give you an idea of how quickly and easily a company or practice can pay its bills.

Working Capital

Working capital measures the firm's ability to pay its bills on time. The larger the working capital, the larger the cushion the firm has should an unexpected downturn in revenue occur. To calculate working capital, simply subtract the current liabilities from the current assets. What's left over is the amount of cash you have if a surprise happens. It's a good measure of short-term liquidity.

$$\text{Working Capital} = \text{Current Assets} - \text{Current Liabilities}$$

Current Ratio

The current ratio is an important tool to assess the firm's ability to pay its bills on time. It gives an idea of the likelihood that the company can pay its bills by comparing its current assets to its current liabilities. For example, if the company had to sell all of its liquid assets, would that be enough to cover all the liabilities due within a year? A general rule of thumb is to have a number higher than 2.0. A ratio of less than 1.0 indicates potential or looming cash flow problems, particularly if unforeseen disruptions in revenue or A/R occur. Bankers, lenders, and even investors will be very wary of any number close to 1.0 and might avoid anything less than 1.0.

$$\text{Current Ratio} = \frac{\text{Current Assets}}{\text{Current Liabilities}}$$

Quick Ratio (Acid Test)

The quick ratio is similar to the current ratio except that it excludes inventory. It measures the firm's ability to pay its bills quickly if needed. A good rule of thumb for this ratio is a target of 0.7–1.1. A higher ratio might indicate a poor use of the firm's assets while a lower ratio might indicate potential cash flow problems.

$$\text{Quick Ratio} = \frac{\text{Cash} + \text{Net A/R} + \text{Short-term Investments}}{\text{Current Liabilities}}$$

Cash Flow to Current Liabilities Ratio

This ratio measures the firm's ability to pay its bills with cash derived from operations. The target for this ratio varies among industries, but a good target is anything greater than 1.0. If this number is less than 1.0, then you've more debt due within one year than you have cash coming into the practice. Keep in mind that this ratio is a snapshot, a specific period in time. If there is seasonality in your revenue, this number will move with it.

$$\text{Cash Flow:Current Liabilities} = \frac{\text{Cash Flows from Operations}}{\text{Current Liabilities}}$$

Free Cash Flow

Free cash flow evaluates the firm's ability to generate surplus cash. It is derived by subtracting capital expenditures and dividend expenses from cash generated from operations. This number may vary across industries, but it should be positive.

Free Cash Flow = Cash from Operations - Capital Expenditures - Dividends

Other Points to Consider

As with most things in accounting, the reports and numbers can be massaged into whatever you want them to be. Here are a few points to consider when looking at liquidity.

What are your available lines of credit? If you have large lines that are untapped, your liquidity might be better than what is represented by these calculations. However, you will alter your balance sheet if you use them. Perhaps you have a few long-term assets you might be able to sell quickly. That's great, but what are those assets being used for? Are they part of your operations? What revenue do they generate?

Finally, some items might not be listed on the reports and therefore not considered in the ratio analysis. An example might be a pending lawsuit that you might lose. If the judgment falls in the other party's favor, then you've got a liability on the books. This is particularly important if you're buying another business or purchasing ownership in a company or practice. You need to perform your due diligence and discover hidden pitfalls like this.

30 | Utilization Ratios

Utilization ratios examine the firm's ability to use its assets in an efficient and productive manner. They can tell you if the practice is using its assets well or poorly.

Inventory Turnover

Inventory turnover examines the firm's ability to "sell out" of its inventory. How long does the product sit on the shelf? This is an indicator of how well the firm can convert its inventory into cash or receivables. Longer times are not desired because revenue is not generated until the product is sold. This is a little more difficult to measure in service industries. However, if you are going to invest in a company that carries inventory, this is a number you might want to look at. If you don't carry inventory in your business, it's doubtful you'll use this. However, if you are investing in a company or purchasing stock, you will want to know this number.

$$\text{Inventory Turnover} = \frac{\text{Cost of Goods Sold}}{\text{Average Inventory}}$$

Days in Inventory

Days in inventory measures how long an item sits on the shelf. It is an indicator of how well the firm can convert its inventory into cash or receivables. Lower times are better; this indicates that a firm can quickly convert inventory into cash. You probably won't use this number in healthcare, but we can make some analogies.

How quickly are you running through your supplies? Are you carrying too much at any given time? Cash invested in supplies and inventory is sitting on a shelf waiting to be used or sold. If it doesn't get used or sold, then perhaps you might want to look at different ways to invest that cash.

$$\text{Days in Inventory} = \frac{365 \text{ Days}}{\text{Inventory Turnover Ratio}}$$

Accounts Receivable Turnover

A/R turnover measures how many times a firm "cashes out" of its receivables for a given period. Higher numbers are desired and indicate that the firm can quickly convert receivables into cash. This is a very important number in healthcare and should be watched by everyone. Getting your money quickly is incredibly important. Days in A/R is another very important ratio to monitor.

$$\text{A/R Turnover} = \frac{\text{Net Sales}}{\text{Average Net A/R}}$$

Days in A/R

Days in A/R measures the length of time it takes for a firm to convert a receivable into cash. In other words, how quickly can it get the money it's owed? Lower numbers indicate faster collection processes and are what we should be aiming for.

You must monitor this number on a regular basis. If it goes up, why? Are claims being submitted late? Is the payer dragging their feet? Do they deny more claims? If the number goes down, why? Did you implement a new coding, billing, or collection system? Or are your people writing off more bad debt? Are they giving up on collecting your money? Look for the trend and always ask why it is occurring.

$$\text{Days in A/R} = \frac{365 \text{ Days}}{\text{A/R Turnover Ratio}}$$

Accounts Payable Turnover

Accounts payable turnover measures the number of times the firm "pays out" its payables. In other words, how quickly does the firm pay its bills? Higher numbers indicate an increasing ability to pay off payables. However, if the number gets too high, are you paying your bills too soon? Could that cash be invested elsewhere for greater returns?

$$\text{A/P Turnover} = \frac{\text{Cost of Goods Sold}}{\text{Average Net A/P}}$$

Days in Accounts Payable

This metric measures the length of time a firm takes to pay off a line of credit or account. There is a balance between how much cash you have and how quickly you pay your bills. This number will vary by industry, but most bills are net 30 (due in 30 days). Bear in mind how your vendors will feel if you take too long to pay them and how it might affect future terms and responsiveness on their part. If you take a long time to pay them, they might demand cash up front instead of terms of payment.

$$\text{Days in A/P} = \frac{365 \text{ Days}}{\text{A/P Turnover Ratio}}$$

Operating Cycle

The operating cycle measures the firm's investment in non-interest-bearing assets. The larger the number, the longer it takes to convert an inventory purchase into cash. It is an indicator of efficient use of assets. Larger numbers indicate a less efficient use of the company's assets.

$$\text{Operating Cycle} = \text{Days in A/R} + \text{Days in Inventory}$$

Cash Conversion Cycle

This is the net position in non-interest-bearing assets versus non-interest-bearing liabilities. It compares the wait time for cash to come into the firm to the wait time to pay its bills. Is the firm waiting for cash, or are the firm's vendors waiting for cash? Are you waiting for your cash, or are you waiting to pay your bills?

$$\text{Cash Conversion Cycle} = \text{Days in A/R} + \text{Days in Inventory} - \text{Days in A/P}$$

Asset Turnover

Asset turnover measures how productive the firm's assets are. It reflects how efficient the assets are at earning cash. This metric looks at the total assets of the company and includes fixed assets as well as current assets. A higher number is always better while the number may vary from industry to industry.

$$\text{Asset Turnover} = \frac{\text{Sales}}{\text{Average Total Sales}}$$

Property, Plant, and Equipment Turnover

This measures how effectively and efficiently your fixed assets are generating income for the firm. It's your revenue divided by the fixed assets on the balance sheet. If you don't have fixed assets (like a hospital-based practice such as a radiology group or hospitalist practice), then this ratio won't be useful for you.

$$\text{PPE Turnover} = \frac{\text{Sales}}{\text{Value of Fixed Assets}}$$

31 | Profitability Ratios

Profitability ratios allow you to quickly ascertain how profitable the business or business unit is at earning cash. These are probably the most common ratios. You'll frequently hear analysts on CNBC or Bloomberg use one or more of these ratios as they discuss the financial future of a particular company. These ratios will tell you how well you manage expenses and create revenue. But remember, when are you recognizing the revenue and what assumptions are you using when recording expenses?

Gross Profit Margin

The gross profit margin is a measure of the success of the pricing strategy of the firm. A higher number is better while the benchmark will vary for industries. The GPM shows how profitable your product or service is. Remember, gross profit is your net sales less cost of services. GPM is typically reported as a percentage or as a dollar figure per $1 of sales.

$$\text{Gross Profit Margin} = \frac{\text{Gross Profit}}{\text{Net Sales}}$$

This is an important metric to watch and track trends over time. If you begin to see this ratio shrink, it's probably costing you more to provide your services, or you've cut your prices to get more business. Either way, you will need to investigate why the ratio is changing.

Operating Profit Margin

Operating profit margin (OPM) is a measure of how successful the daily operations of the practice are at earning cash. Operating profit, or EBIT, is net sales less operating expenses. Operating profit margin is a percentage of how much of your income from operations comes from your net sales or revenue. Higher numbers are desired. Operating margin is typically expressed as a percentage.

$$\text{Operating Margin} = \frac{\text{Income from Operations}}{\text{Net Sales}}$$

Again, if this number begins to decline, investigate. Are costs rising faster than charges? Have you agreed to a charge reduction to get more business? Always investigate trend changes.

Net Profit Margin

The net profit margin (NPM) is how much of every dollar the company keeps after it has paid all of its bills. It is also known as *return on sales*. Net profit margin is the bottom-line ratio of the bottom line number. Keep in mind that interest and taxes play a role in this number, not just the operational costs of the company. When trying to manage this number, understand what you can and cannot control. If you're having someone else manage your business, realize they probably can't control taxes or interest paid. Only you or the c-suite can do that. It will likely be up to the owners to make financial decisions that affect taxes and interest.

$$\text{Net Profit Margin} = \frac{\text{Net Income}}{\text{Net Sales}}$$

Return on Assets

Return on assets (ROA) measures how efficiently the firm uses its assets to earn cash. Said another way, this is the percentage of every dollar invested into the company that has come back in the form of revenue. A higher number is desired. However, this number can be driven higher if those assets used to generate revenue aren't being replaced when their useful life is over. If that happens, watch your working capital and other ratios to make certain you can afford to fix or replace the asset when it stops working. Otherwise, your revenue will take a hit as you scramble to replace the asset.

$$\text{ROA} = \frac{\text{Net Income}}{\text{Total Assets}}$$

Return on Equity

Return on equity (ROE) is how much each dollar invested into the company is making in revenue. This is different from the assets used by the company to make money. Equity can fluctuate according to the accounting equation. If you have more liabilities and have structured your financing that way, then your ROE might be higher than the company that decided to sell shares to raise cash instead of taking out a loan. You will usually compare this rate to what you might earn out in the market in other investments, such as T-bills or the average Dow returns.

$$\text{ROE} = \frac{\text{Net Income}}{\text{Total Equity}}$$

EBITDA

Earnings before interest, taxes, depreciation, and amortization (EBITDA) measures the profitability of the firm. This metric filters out the financing and accounting decisions of the firm. Decisions on purchasing, borrowing, and taxes are not included in an attempt to look more closely at the real profitability of the firm. EBITDA is a measure of profitability but not cash flow. Keeping that point in mind is important. EBITDA also ignores cash needed to fund working capital. It is a good number to compare to your net profit margin, as the difference in these two can give you insight into the financing and accounting decisions you have made.

EBITDA = Revenue - Expenses (excluding Interest, Taxes, Depreciation, and Amortization)

Operating Expense Ratio

Operating expense measures how successfully a firm manages its expenses. It's the portion of net sales that goes into running the company and generating those sales or revenues. A lower ratio is better and desired.

$$\text{Operating Expense} = \frac{\text{Total Operating Expense}}{\text{Net Sales}}$$

Dividend Payout

This measures how much profit a firm returns to the owners in cash. It's an indication of the money a company is returning to their shareholders instead of keeping it to reinvest in the company, pay down debt, or hold for a rainy day. This ratio isn't likely to be used by a practice, but if you're investing in another company, it's a good number to watch.

$$\text{Dividend Payout} = \frac{\text{Cash Dividends}}{\text{Net Income}}$$

Earnings Per Share

Earnings per share (EPS) measures the profit earned per share issued by the firm. It is the only ratio usually reported on a financial statement. Higher ratios are desired, particularly if you're a shareholder.

$$EPS = \frac{Net\ Income}{Total\ Number\ of\ Shares}$$

Price to Earnings Ratio

The price to earnings ratio (P/E ratio) measures the stock market's view of the firm. Keep in mind that the denominator is an annual measurement. Therefore, it is the stock price of one share divided by the annual earnings of that share. It can then be stated that the result is how many years it will take to reclaim the cost of the share of stock.

$$P/E\ Ratio = \frac{Stock\ Market\ Share\ Price}{EPS}$$

Price to Book Value

Price to book value (P/B) is a measure of the market's value of the firm to the firm's value of the firm. It's a way of comparing what the market thinks the company is worth to what the financial reports say it's worth.

$$P/B\ Ratio = \frac{Stock\ Market\ Share\ Price}{Book\ Value\ per\ Share}$$

32 | Financial Strength Ratios

Financial strength (or solvency) ratios relate to how strong the firm is in a financial sense. In today's world of unknown delays in revenue receipt, you must know how healthy your company is if you are to survive any bumps in the road ahead.

The following ratios will give you an idea of how leveraged your company is. Debt isn't a bad thing or a good thing. It's merely a tool to use if you're short on cash or want to raise cash for a capital expenditure. Remember, net income is after you've paid all taxes and interest, and you pay interest before you pay taxes. So from a tax point of view, a capital structure that utilizes debt can help reduce your tax liability.

Debt to Equity

The Debit to Equity (D/E) ratio measures the firm's total liabilities by the stockholder's equity. It shows how much debt the company has for every dollar the investors have given the company. Higher ratios are riskier and can vary greatly from industry to industry. It can also be viewed as the balance between the two sources of capital—creditors and owners. As mentioned before, interest paid on debt is deductible from taxes. It's not uncommon for a company to carry some debt. This is an important ratio to watch, particularly if you're seeking to raise cash via debt. Bankers will take a close look at this number to determine the risk they will face should they loan you money.

$$\text{D/E Ratio} = \frac{\text{Total Liabilities}}{\text{Stockholders' Equity}}$$

Total Debt/Total Asset Ratios

The total debt to total asset ratio is a good indicator of the capital financing structure of the company. This ratio is also known as the debt ratio. This ratio reports the percentage of assets funded by debt. A higher number is riskier. If this number is high, check the equity section of the balance sheet because it might be getting smaller.

$$\text{TD/TA} = \frac{\text{Total Debt}}{\text{Total Assets}}$$

Times Interest Earned

Times interest earned (TIE) measures how easily the interest expense can be funded by the profits of the firm. It's also sometimes referred to as interest coverage. Lower ratios are riskier and indicate the firm might have trouble meeting its interest obligations. This is another important ratio for banks because it shows how likely it is that they will be paid. An important point to keep in mind is that lease payments will not show up in this ratio or any debt ratio. Those expenses appear on the income statement and do not show up on a balance sheet. The company still has recurring obligations for the lease and is bound by the lease they signed. The investor or banker will have to examine the income statement to see what the company's expenses really are.

$$\text{TIE} = \frac{\text{Income Before Interest and Taxes}}{\text{Interest Expense}}$$

Debt to Capitalization Ratio

This ratio measures what role debt plays in the organization's operation and growth. How much is the organization relying on debt to support its operations and growth? A lower number is better, indicating a low dependency upon debt by the firm.

$$\text{Debt:Capitalization Ratio} = \frac{\text{Long-term Debt}}{\text{Long-term Debt} + \text{Stockholder Equity}}$$

33 | Payer Mix and Productivity Metrics

Payer Mix

Payer mix is an important item to consider. Using a weighted average of the payers, the physician can budget and plan for the future. It is important to know what type of coverage your patients are carrying and what percentage of your practice is represented by them.

Below is an example, Figure 3.1, of a payer mix report.

Figure 3.1 - Payer Mix Report

Payer	# Visits	% visits
Other Contractual	686	6.5%
Aetna	203	1.9%
BC/BS	1,801	16.9%
Cigna	81	0.8%
Coventry	1,303	12.3%
Medicare	3,420	32.1%
PHS	766	7.2%
PPK	1,027	9.7%
United	877	8.2%
WPPA	92	0.9%
Non-contractual	382	3.6%

Reviewing this report on a monthly basis is incredibly important. It can provide valuable data regarding volume and which payers' subscribers are using your services. After you create the payer mix report, look at the days in A/R for each payer. Which payer is paying you the fastest? Which is paying the slowest? Why? Is the issue on your side or theirs? What can you do to get more of the better, faster-paying payer's patients? Who are your largest payers? Who are your smallest? Also, know when your contracts are coming up for renewal. Use this data as you begin to prepare for your next round of negotiations.

Productivity Metrics

Productivity metrics are important. They give insight into how the organization is performing, the need for manpower, and ways to increase revenue and decrease costs. This discussion touches on the operational control of a practice. Operations and finance are intertwined. Operations (the processes of your practice) will have their own metrics to follow. However, the outcomes of those operations are reflected in the financial metrics and reports.

We use financial reports and ratios to determine how successful our process improvement efforts are. Most operational cost savings initiatives will have financial metrics attached to them. There are times we use productivity metrics such as visits per day or cancelations per day. However, the ultimate test is whether or not the process changes impacted the financial reports.

You have several productivity metrics to choose from. Just pick the ones that work best for you and, more importantly, that you can control.

Office Visits

Office visits are important for any medical practice. Whether the visit occurs in the office, at the patient's home, or via the web, seeing patients is the reason we are in business. Physicians of America sees patients for a variety of reasons. New patients, established patients, hospital visits, and nursing home visits all make up parts of their revenue.

Knowing how much time it takes to see each patient is critical for effective and efficient scheduling. There is a fine balance between spending enough time with patients to discover their real problems and being too focused on productivity. We need to spend time communicating with the patient if we are to help them improve their health. Some patients communicate slower than others. We want to balance our desire to help them with being efficient. Avoid being so focused on efficiency that you lose sight of the reason you're in practice—helping others.

Procedures

What type of procedures are you performing? How many are you performing? You might look at your procedures per day or procedures per visit. Then you might look at average revenue per procedure. You will want to know what you generate with each type of procedure. Also, how long does a procedure take on average? I've found that most people think they are faster than they really are. It can be painful, but examine how much time you're spending on each procedure. Finally, establish and monitor a quality metric for each procedure. What are you good at? What could you improve?

Consultations

Office visits and in-hospital consultations will be important for you to monitor. Who is sending you patients? What type of patient are they typically sending you? How often do they give you referrals? What are the trends? What can you do to improve them?

Relative Value Units

I will address relative value units (RVUs) in Part 4. You will need a good understanding of how these are calculated and used. They are fundamental to many service agreements.

Charges

Charges are what you charge for your services. Reviewing your monthly gross charges is important. It can be an indicator of productivity and how busy you were. It can also give you an idea of how much cash you will have coming into the practice over the next few weeks or months. Net charges will be the amount you charge after you apply your contractual write-offs.

Collections

Charges are important, but collections are more important because that is money you've actually received. It's how much cash you've received for your services. Watch your collections very closely and, as always, ask questions when things don't make sense.

34

Ratios for the Medical Practice

In this chapter, I would like to spend some time discussing the more common and important ratios and metrics you might use in a medical practice.

Collection Ratio

The collection ratio is a look at your ability to negotiate with payers. It measures your contractual adjustments on your overall earnings. How much money do you actually collect for every dollar you bill for? A lower number is desired. However, a lower number doesn't really mean much if you're a poor negotiator or aren't charging enough to begin with. The equation is:

$$\text{Collection Ratio} = \frac{\text{Gross Charges}}{\text{Net Collections}}$$

Days in A/R

Days in A/R has already been discussed, but it would be good to revisit this important metric again here. Let's assume you've generated $500,000 in total charges over the past quarter, or 90 days. The total amount you're still owed, your A/R balance, is $400,000.

To find how long it takes you to collect, we perform the following calculations. First, we calculate your daily revenue rate.

$$\frac{\$500,000}{90 \text{ days}} = \$5,555/\text{day}$$

Next, we take your current A/R balance and divide by your daily revenue rate to find your days in A/R.

$$\frac{\$400,000}{\$5,555/\text{day}} = 72 \text{ days in A/R}$$

In this example, it takes you about 72 days to collect on your outstanding A/R balances. This is a very important number. Because as we saw earlier, timing is everything. If your days in A/R is 72 days, then you will want either 72 days of cash or liquid assets on hand or have access to a revolving line of credit to cover your expenses while you wait to get paid.

Expense to Charges Revenue Ratio

There are a number of ways to get a meaningful number that relates to your expense to earnings ratio or your overhead expense ratio. The first method is to take your total operating expenses and divide it by the total revenue of the practice. The total operating expenses usually include your overhead less the salaries and benefits of the providers. The revenue number is determined by the total collections or net collections if you're using a cash basis method of accounting.

$$\frac{\text{Total Operating Expenses}}{\text{Total Revenue}} = \text{Overhead as a Percentage of Revenue}$$

Another method of getting a valuable number is using the same equation, but this time including all of your expenses in the operating expenses. You would include your providers' salaries and benefits in the total expenses number. Using both will give you an idea of how much of your overhead is people and how much is other stuff. It's a good idea to perform both calculations and watch them over time.

Visits per Provider per Day

This is a pretty simple and straightforward metric. How many patients does each provider see in a day? It's a measure of productivity. However, you might want to get a little more detailed and examine the level of encounters for each provider. Does one particular provider see more complex patients than another?

Staffing Ratios

These ratios are different in that they do not address expenses or dollars, but rather examine how efficiently the practice uses its providers and staff.

To get an idea of your staffing ratio, use the following equation.

$$\frac{\text{Total \# of FTEs}}{\text{Total \# of Providers}} = \text{Staffing Ratio}$$

The total number of providers would include physicians and mid-level providers. Anyone who generates a professional charge should be included in the denominator. The total of full-time equivalents (FTE) would include those employees and staff who are needed in the clinic but do not generate charges (LPNs, RNs, and the like). These numbers are useful as they give insight into your operations and the efficiency of your practice.

It's important to keep in mind that with a staffing ratio of 2.0, each provider must generate enough revenue to cover the costs of not only 2.0 FTEs but also their own salary.

Here are some other examples of staffing ratios you might use:

- Number of non-medical staff members per provider

- Total staff members per provider
- Encounter ratios

Knowing how much you earn for each patient you see is necessary for budgeting and forecasting. A common number you might use is your average revenue per patient seen. It's very simple to calculate this ratio. You will want to match your revenue period with your productivity period, say, the first quarter or the month of May.

$$\frac{\text{Total Revenue}}{\text{Total \# of Patients Seen}} = \text{Average Revenue per Patient}$$

You can use this ratio to dive deeper into your various service lines and providers. You might look at average revenue per patient per provider, or average revenue per patient per insurance carrier type. Whichever way you want to look at the data is fine—just make sure you look at the data.

We cannot talk about revenue without also talking about expenses or costs. Here too, you can look at your average cost per patient. Once you have these two numbers, you can get a good idea of your profitability and viability in the future. The revenue ratio gives an indication of your charges, and the expense ratio will be an early warning sign of rising costs.

To find your average cost per patient, instead of putting your total revenue in the numerator, put your total expenses in.

$$\frac{\text{Total Expenses}}{\text{Total \# of Patients Seen}} = \text{Average Expense per Patient}$$

Two other ratios that you will want to monitor are your no-show rate and the physician cancelation rate. How frequently are your patients not showing up for their appointments? How frequently are you or another physician canceling their appointments? This is a bigger issue for procedural-based practices such as those in the surgical services. Emergencies will occur and disrupt the best-laid plans. Watching these numbers will give you some guidance in how you should schedule your day.

RVU Ratios

Those who pay for healthcare, basically the federal government, have tried to create a simple and easy way to assign a value to the various services different physicians and specialists provide. Medicare created the relative value units (RVU) system as an attempt to reign in rising healthcare costs. In 1992, the Centers for Medicare and Medicaid Services began to use the Resource-Based Relative Value Scale (RBRVS). It was an attempt to compare apples to apples. Many large groups, hospitals, and practices use RVUs as a way of measuring productivity and creating incentive programs. A common ratio you might encounter is the average RVU per patient visit.

$$\frac{\text{Total \# of Patient Visits}}{\text{Total \# of RVUs}} = \text{Average RVUs per patient visit}$$

You can then do this same calculation for each provider or service line.

Benchmarking

Just like ratios, benchmarks are important to the financial analysis of your practice. What you do here is compare yourself to others in your city, state, region, type of practice, etc. You're basically peeking over the fence to see how your neighbors are doing. Many different organizations provide this data. The Medical Group Management Association (MGMA) has very in-depth reports. The American Medical Group Association (AMGA) also provides various data reports on benchmarking as well. There are private entities such as Cejka, Jackson Healthcare, The Gallup Organization, and Ernst & Young just to name a few. The government has several more reports. These organizations collect and analyze the raw data which are used by healthcare providers, third party payers, hospitals, and the like.

There are some issues with using such data from these firms. First and foremost, the reports are only as good as the data they collect. They rely on practice managers, executives, and physicians to complete their surveys. Not every group or practice will report or define productivity the same. Different groups might decide to include different items in their revenue numbers while excluding items from their expense numbers. It's the same issue we as physicians face when conducting a clinical trial or determining if a study applies to our practice—does the cohort studied match our practice? That's why you should understand how they arrive at their numbers. Don't just accept their benchmarks as a gold standard. You should first be certain their data is applicable.

That being said, there are some very good benchmarks you can use as a guide for your practice. Here are some common productivity benchmarks:

- RVUs per provider
- RVUs per visit
- Gross charges per visit
- Net charges per visit

The list goes on, and you can be as creative or detailed as you like. It's important that you pick the ratios and benchmarks that work for you. Use ones that you can control and change.

35

How Far Off Course Are We?

In healthcare, we have normal values. They are the benchmarks by which we compare our patients' data to determine how healthy they are. There is a normal range for serum potassium or thyroid stimulating hormone. We compare our normal labs to the patients' to determine how much correction is necessary. In accounting, we do the same thing and use the term *variance*. Variance allows us to see trends and changes in the performance of the business. It can be good or bad change, up or down. If we don't watch for it, we won't know when it happens.

For a quick review, variance is the change in a parameter or metric. Percent change can sometimes be more meaningful as we analyze our financial reports. Percent change is calculated by taking the final data point, subtracting the initial data point, and then dividing the difference by the initial data point. You probably do this naturally in your head, but having it on paper where you can see it helps a great deal.

$$Y = a + bX$$

Your accountant or office manager should provide you with percentage changes when comparing one period to another. If they don't, you will have to do it yourself and maybe get a new office manager.

Horizontal and Vertical Analysis

Horizontal Analysis

In horizontal analysis, we compare the line item from one period of time to another.

Let's examine Physicians of America's income statements in Figure 3.2. Looking at it, we see gross charges rose by 6%, and adjustments fell by 4.4%. That seems to be a move in the right direction. However, the personnel expenses rose by 22% which accounts for the majority of the rise in their operating expenses. This is a big red flag and should be investigated.

Why did personnel expenses rise? Did they hire more people? Did the cost of employment rise? What explains this spike? Looking at the rest of the income statement, we see total expenses rose by 7.3% while total overhead fell by 16.3%. Again, the culprit appears to be personnel costs. Finally, we see their net profit dropped by 14.4%. This is quite concerning and should prompt POA to look for new ways to generate revenue, negotiate new rates with payers, and look for cost savings.

Looking at POA's balance sheet in Figure 3.3, we observe that cash didn't change in a substantial manner, and yet patient A/R rose by 12.8%. That's a big bump. What explains this? Is it their collection and billing process? Is it the economy? The new healthcare plans? Until they rule out what they can change, they shouldn't just accept whatever theory they believe to be the answer. It might be the economy, but POA should investigate their processes to ensure they are as efficient and effective as possible. The rule is to fix what you can, and accept what you can't.

We also notice that POA's liabilities grew by 70%. That kind of growth should be concerning. Why did they need to use the line of credit? What issues are they facing that have caused them to use the line of credit? Again, focus on what you can fix.

Figure 3.2 - Horizontal Analysis of Income Statements

Income Statement Horizontal Analysis

for years ending

		12/31/14		12/31/15	
Gross Charges:					
Professional Service Charges	$	1,139,223	$	1,275,745	11.98%
Orthopedic Charges	$	9,101	$	8,143	-10.52%
Injection Charges	$	101,941	$	105,328	3.32%
Immunization Charges	$	147,206	$	104,298	-29.15%
Procedure Charges	$	115,860	$	115,725	-0.12%
Laboratory Charges	$	728,329	$	711,383	-2.33%
Radiology Charges	$	122,113	$	125,539	2.81%
Hospital Charges	$	84,383	$	124,821	47.92%
Nursing Home Charges	$	20,061	$	46,825	133.42%
Miscellaneous Charges	$	3,375	$	2,364	-29.97%
Gross Charges Total:	$	**2,471,593**	$	**2,620,171**	6.01%
Contractual Adjustments:					
Other Contractual Adjustments	$	(65,177)	$	(60,735)	-6.82%
Aetna Adjustments	$	(19,267)	$	(27,489)	42.67%
BC/BS Adjustments	$	(171,064)	$	(159,398)	-6.82%
Cigna Adjustments	$	(7,651)	$	(6,323)	-17.36%
Coventry Adjustments	$	(123,789)	$	(120,066)	-3.01%
Medicare Adjustments	$	(324,835)	$	(350,185)	7.80%
PHS Adjustments	$	(72,798)	$	(68,449)	-5.97%
PPK Adjustments	$	(97,514)	$	(52,775)	-45.88%
United Adjustments	$	(83,310)	$	(93,140)	11.80%
WPPA Adjustments	$	(8,749)	$	(12,683)	44.97%
Non-contractual Adjustments	$	(36,277)	$	(17,071)	-52.94%
Pre-paid Contract Adj. - PPK	$	(73,886)	$	(69,932)	-5.35%
Refunds	$	(37,503)	$	(28,552)	-23.87%
Contractual Adjustments Total:	$	**(1,121,820)**	$	**(1,066,797)**	-4.90%
Net Medical Charges:	$	**1,349,773**	$	**1,553,374**	15.08%
Capitation Revenue	$	121,245	$	138,231	14.01%
Other Operating Income	$	65,262	$	43,901	-32.73%
Adj to Cash Collections	$	259,478	$	160,886	-38.00%
Total Net Revenue:	$	**1,795,757**	$	**1,896,391**	5.60%

Expenses

Total Professional Exp	$	189,703	$	242,661	27.92%
Total EE Exp	$	398,454	$	466,552	17.09%
Total Physician Sal/Ben	$	11,339	$	22,741	100.56%
Total Personnel Expense	$	599,496	$	731,954	22.09%
Comp Equip < $500	$	346	$	137	-60.40%
Comp Equip Maint	$	20,894	$	12,967	-37.94%
Comp Equip / Dep Exp	$	689	$	2,024	193.76%
Total Computer Expense	$	21,928	$	15,128	-31.01%
Radiology Supplies	$	-	$	-	
Outside Radiology Fees	$	21,008	$	22,766	8.37%
Radiology Equip Lease/Rent	$	-	$	-	
Radiology Equip Maint	$	7,754	$	3,390	-56.28%
Other Radiology Exp	$	222	$	2,058	827.03%
Total Radiology Expense	$	28,984	$	28,214	-2.66%
Lab Supplies	$	49,250	$	47,997	-2.54%
Outside Lab Fees	$	21,051	$	20,724	-1.55%
Lab Equip Lease / Rent	$	9,812	$	9,751	-0.62%
Lab Equip Maint	$	2,438	$	7,444	205.33%
Other Lab Exp	$	6,517	$	5,969	-8.41%
Total Laboratory Exp	$	89,069	$	91,885	3.16%
Biohazard Waste	$	3,930	$	4,624	17.66%
Building Lease	$	220,391	$	222,711	1.05%
Janitorial Services	$	8,554	$	8,591	0.43%
Total Building Exp	$	232,875	$	235,926	1.31%
Drugs & Meds	$	86,116	$	72,258	-16.09%
Medical Supp	$	15,030	$	25,159	67.39%
Office Supplies	$	6,751	$	6,788	0.55%
Laundry & Linen	$	4,485	$	3,984	-11.17%
Janitorial Supp	$	2,506	$	2,499	-0.28%
Total Supplies Expense	$	114,887	$	110,688	-3.65%
Total Operating Expenses	$	1,087,239	$	1,213,795	11.64%

Furn / Equip Lease	$	3,151	$ 3,316	5.24%
Property Tax Furn / Equip	$	278	$ 201	-27.70%
Insurance Furn / Equip	$	1,779	$ 2,680	50.65%
Maint / Repairs Furn / Equip	$	2,218	$ 2,409	8.61%
Small Tools & Equip	$	258	$ 1,199	364.73%
Total Furn / Equip Exp	$	7,685	$ 9,805	27.59%
Legal Fees	$	2,333	$ 1,117	-52.12%
Accounting Fees	$	2,195	$ 889	-59.50%
Collection Svcs	$	-	$ -	
Other Purchased Svcs	$	25,267	$ 19,729	-21.92%
Transcription Svcs	$	-	$ -	
Storage Exp	$	50	$ 50	0.00%
Total Purchased Svcs	$	29,846	$ 21,785	-27.01%
Recruitment	$	231	$ 786	240.26%
Employee Relations	$	533	$ 568	6.57%
Prof Liability Insurance	$	21,252	$ 24,609	15.80%
Total EE Related Svcs	$	22,016	$ 25,963	17.93%
Telephone Exp	$	10,933	$ 10,104	-7.58%
Prof Listings / Promo	$	12,095	$ 11,778	-2.62%
Postage & Freight	$	8,095	$ 8,537	5.46%
Bank Fees	$	9,241	$ 10,884	17.78%
Books, Subscrip, Etc.	$	890	$ 546	-38.65%
Other G&A Exp	$	18	$ 37	105.56%
Total Gen & Adm Exp	$	41,272	$ 41,886	1.49%
Non-Op Rev/Exp	$	71,493	$ 44,702	-37.47%
Total Overhead	$	172,312	$ 144,141	-16.35%
Total Expenses	$	1,259,551	$ 1,357,936	7.81%
Net Profit	$	536,206	$ 538,455	0.42%

Figure 3.3 - Horizontal Analysis of Balance Sheet

Balance Sheet Horiztonal Analysis

	Dec 31, 2014	Dec 31, 2015	
Current Assets			
Cash in Bank	$ 23,139	$ 28,602	23.61%
Savings Acct	$ 59,725	$ 61,792	3.46%
Patients Receivable	$ 251,944	$ 284,160	12.79%
Accounts Receivable-Bldg	$ 95,065	$ 95,065	0.00%
Receipts Not Posted	$ (164)	$ (164)	-0.19%
Pre-aid Insurance			
Investment Receivables	$ 2,600	$ 1,200	-53.85%
Total Current Assets	**$ 432,309**	**$ 470,655**	8.87%
Fixed Assets			
Furniture & Fixtures	$ 219,624	$ 219,624	0.00%
Software	$ 64,093	$ 64,093	0.00%
Accumulated Depreciation	$ (266,147)	$ (280,246)	5.30%
Total Property & Equipment	**$ 17,570**	**$ 3,471**	-80.24%
Other Assets			
Organizational Costs	$ 3,406	$ 3,406	-0.01%
Accumulated Amortization	$ (3,406)	$ (3,406)	-0.01%
Utility Deposit	$ 3,215	$ 3,215	0.01%
Inv-TI	$ 5,111	$ 3,444	-32.62%
Total Other Assets	**$ 8,326**	**$ 6,659**	-20.02%
Total Assets	**$ 458,205**	**$ 480,786**	4.93%
Current Liabilities			
Loans Payable—Line Of Credit	$ 44,274	$ 113,702	156.81%
Loans Payable—Malpractice			
Loans Payable—Furniture, Furnishings, and Equipmer	$ 31,341	$ 14,714	-53.05%
FUTA Tax Payable	$ 31	$ 32	3.23%
SUTA Tax Payable	$ 40	$ 39	-3.31%
Total Current Liabilities	**$ 75,686**	**$ 128,487**	69.76%
Deferred Revenue			
Deferred Accounts Receivable	$ 254,883	$ 253,635	-0.49%
Total Liabilities	**$ 330,569**	**$ 382,122**	15.60%
Members' Capital			
Retained Earnings	$ 53,700	$ 50,557	-5.85%
Members' Capital Accounts	$ 25,470	$ 57,660	126.38%
Members' Curr Yr Capital Contrib.	$ 1,500	$ 3,613	140.87%
General Draws	$ (430,445)	$ (519,886)	20.78%
Draws—Health, Dental	$ (14,574)	$ (9,340)	-35.91%
Draws—Life & Disability Ins.	$ (6,128)	$ (3,103)	-49.37%
Draws—401(K) Deferral	$ (38,093)	$ (19,292)	-49.36%
Current Yr Net Income	$ 536,206	$ 538,455	0.42%
Total Members' Capital	**$ 127,636**	**$ 98,664**	-22.70%
Total Liabilities & Capital	**$ 458,205**	**$ 480,786**	4.93%

Vertical Analysis

In vertical analysis, we look at each item as a percentage of the total classification it is in.

Examining the gross charges for POA in Figure 3.4, we see that 48.7% of gross charges were for professional services rendered. This grew by almost 3% from the prior year. We also notice that lab dropped and now comprises a smaller percentage of charges. Professional expenses represent 60% of their total operating expenses.

The balance sheet in Figure 3.5 tells an interesting story. Of all their assets, patient A/R is the largest asset totaling 62.5% of their current assets and just a hair less of their total assets. We should allow for a percentage of this asset that they will not collect. But the important thing to know is where the assets are on the balance sheet in relation to one another.

Figure 3.4 - Vertical Analysis of Income Statement

Income Statement Vertical Analysis

for years ending

	12/31/14		12/31/15	
Gross Charges:				
Professional Service Charges	$ 1,139,223	46.09%	$ 1,275,745	48.69%
Orthopedic Charges	$ 9,101	0.37%	$ 8,143	0.31%
Injection Charges	$ 101,941	4.12%	$ 105,328	4.02%
Immunization Charges	$ 147,206	5.96%	$ 104,298	3.98%
Procedure Charges	$ 115,860	4.69%	$ 115,725	4.42%
Laboratory Charges	$ 728,329	29.47%	$ 711,383	27.15%
Radiology Charges	$ 122,113	4.94%	$ 125,539	4.79%
Hospital Charges	$ 84,383	3.41%	$ 124,821	4.76%
Nursing Home Charges	$ 20,061	0.81%	$ 46,825	1.79%
Miscellaneous Charges	$ 3,375	0.14%	$ 2,364	0.09%
Gross Charges Total:	**$ 2,471,593**	100.00%	**$ 2,620,171**	100.00%
Contractual Adjustments:				
Other Contractual Adjustments	$ (65,177)	5.81%	$ (60,735)	5.69%
Aetna Adjustments	$ (19,267)	1.72%	$ (27,489)	2.58%
BC/BS Adjustments	$ (171,064)	15.25%	$ (159,398)	14.94%
Cigna Adjustments	$ (7,651)	0.68%	$ (6,323)	0.59%
Coventry Adjustments	$ (123,789)	11.03%	$ (120,066)	11.25%
Medicare Adjustments	$ (324,835)	28.96%	$ (350,185)	32.83%
PHS Adjustments	$ (72,798)	6.49%	$ (68,449)	6.42%
PPK Adjustments	$ (97,514)	8.69%	$ (52,775)	4.95%
United Adjustments	$ (83,310)	7.43%	$ (93,140)	8.73%
WPPA Adjustments	$ (8,749)	0.78%	$ (12,683)	1.19%
Non-contractual Adjustments	$ (36,277)	3.23%	$ (17,071)	1.60%
		0.00%		0.00%
Pre-paid Contract Adj. - PPK	$ (73,886)	6.59%	$ (69,932)	6.56%
Refunds	$ (37,503)	3.34%	$ (28,552)	2.68%
Contractual Adjustments Total:	**$ (1,121,820)**	100.00%	**$ (1,066,797)**	100.00%
Net Medical Charges:	**$ 1,349,773**		**$ 1,553,374**	
Capitation Revenue	$ 121,245	6.80%	$ 138,231	7.60%
Other Operating Income	$ 65,262	3.60%	$ 43,901	2.40%
Adj to Cash Collections	$ 259,478	14.40%	$ 160,886	8.90%
Total Net Revenue:	**$ 1,795,757**	100.00%	**$ 1,896,391**	100.00%

Expenses

Total Professional Exp	$	189,703	17.40% $	242,661	20.10%
Total EE Exp	$	398,454	36.60% $	466,552	38.60%
Total Physician Sal/Ben	$	11,339	1.00% $	22,741	1.90%
Total Personnel Expense	$	599,496	55.10% $	731,954	60.60%
Comp Equip < $500	$	346	0.00% $	137	0.00%
Comp Equip Maint	$	20,894	1.90% $	12,967	1.10%
Comp Equip / Dep Exp	$	689	0.10% $	2,024	0.20%
Total Computer Expense	$	21,928	2.00% $	15,128	1.30%
Radiology Supplies	$	-	0.00% $	-	0.00%
Outside Radiology Fees	$	21,008	1.90% $	22,766	1.90%
Radiology Equip Lease/Rent	$	-	0.00% $	-	0.00%
Radiology Equip Maint	$	7,754	0.70% $	3,390	0.30%
Other Radiology Exp	$	222	0.00% $	2,058	0.20%
Total Radiology Expense	$	28,984	2.70% $	28,214	2.30%
Lab Supplies	$	49,250	4.50% $	47,997	4.00%
Outside Lab Fees	$	21,051	1.90% $	20,724	1.70%
Lab Equip Lease / Rent	$	9,812	0.90% $	9,751	0.80%
Lab Equip Maint	$	2,438	0.20% $	7,444	0.60%
Other Lab Exp	$	6,517	0.60% $	5,969	0.50%
Total Laboratory Exp	$	89,069	8.20% $	91,885	7.60%
Biohazard Waste	$	3,930	0.40% $	4,624	0.40%
Building Lease	$	220,391	20.30% $	222,711	18.40%
Janitorial Services	$	8,554	0.80% $	8,591	0.70%
Total Building Exp	$	232,875	21.40% $	235,926	19.50%
Drugs & Meds	$	86,116	7.90% $	72,258	6.00%
Medical Supp	$	15,030	1.40% $	25,159	2.10%
Office Supplies	$	6,751	0.60% $	6,788	0.60%
Laundry & Linen	$	4,485	0.40% $	3,984	0.30%
Janitorial Supp	$	2,506	0.20% $	2,499	0.20%
Total Supplies Expense	$	114,887	10.60% $	110,688	8.70%
Total Operating Expenses	$	1,087,239	100.00% $	1,213,795	100.00%

Furn / Equip Lease	$	3,151	1.80%	$ 3,316	2.30%
Property Tax Furn / Equip	$	278	0.20%	$ 201	0.10%
Insurance Furn / Equip	$	1,779	1.00%	$ 2,680	1.90%
Maint / Repairs Furn / Equip	$	2,218	1.30%	$ 2,409	1.70%
Small Tools & Equip	$	258	0.10%	$ 1,199	0.80%
Total Furn / Equip Exp	$	7,685	4.50%	$ 9,805	6.80%
Legal Fees	$	2,333	1.40%	$ 1,117	0.80%
Accounting Fees	$	2,195	1.30%	$ 889	0.60%
Collection Svcs	$	-	0.00%	$ -	0.00%
Other Purchased Svcs	$	25,267	14.70%	$ 19,729	13.70%
Transcription Svcs	$	-	0.00%	$ -	0.00%
Storage Exp	$	50	0.00%	$ 50	0.00%
Total Purchased Svcs	$	29,846	17.30%	$ 21,785	15.10%
Recruitment	$	231	0.10%	$ 786	0.50%
Employee Relations	$	533	0.30%	$ 568	0.40%
Prof Liability Insurance	$	21,252	12.30%	$ 24,609	17.10%
Total EE Related Svcs	$	22,016	12.80%	$ 25,963	18.00%
Telephone Exp	$	10,933	6.30%	$ 10,104	7.00%
Prof Listings / Promo	$	12,095	7.00%	$ 11,778	8.20%
Postage & Freight	$	8,095	4.70%	$ 8,537	5.90%
Bank Fees	$	9,241	5.40%	$ 10,884	7.60%
Books, Subscrip, Etc.	$	890	0.50%	$ 546	0.40%
Other G&A Exp	$	18	0.00%	$ 37	0.00%
Total Gen & Adm Exp	$	41,272	24.00%	$ 41,886	29.10%
Non-Op Rev/Exp	$	71,493	41.50%	$ 44,702	31.00%
Total Overhead	$	172,312	100.00%	$ 144,141	100.00%
Total Expenses	$	1,259,551		$ 1,357,936	
Net Profit	$	536,206		$ 538,455	

Figure 3.5 - Vertical Analysis of Balance Sheet

Balance Sheet Vertical Analysis

		Dec 31, 2014			Dec 31, 2015	
Current Assets						
	Cash in Bank	$	23,139	5.05% $	28,602	5.95%
	Savings Acct	$	59,725	13.03% $	61,792	12.85%
	Patients Receivable	$	251,944	54.98% $	284,160	59.10%
	Accounts Receivable-Bldg	$	95,065	20.75% $	95,065	19.77%
	Receipts Not Posted	$	(164)	-0.04% $	(164)	-0.03%
	Pre-paid Insurance					
	Investment Receivables	$	2,600	0.57% $	1,200	0.25%
	Total Current Assets	**$**	**432,309**	**94.35% $**	**470,655**	**97.89%**
Fixed Assets						
	Furniture & Fixtures	$	219,624	47.93% $	219,624	45.68%
	Software	$	64,093	13.99% $	64,093	13.33%
	Accumulated Depreciation	$	(266,147)	-58.08% $	(280,246)	-58.29%
	Total Property & Equipment	**$**	**17,570**	**3.83% $**	**3,471**	**0.72%**
Other Assets						
	Organizational Costs	$	3,406	0.74% $	3,406	0.71%
	Accumulated Amortization	$	(3,406)	-0.74% $	(3,406)	-0.71%
	Utility Deposit	$	3,215	0.70% $	3,215	0.67%
	Inv-TI	$	5,111	1.12% $	3,444	0.72%
	Total Other Assets	**$**	**8,326**	**1.82% $**	**6,659**	**1.39%**
	Total Assets	**$**	**458,205**	**100.00% $**	**480,786**	**100.00%**
Current Liabilities						
	Loans Payable—Line Of Credit	$	44,274	13.39% $	113,702	29.76%
	Loans Payable—Malpractice			0.00%		0.00%
	Loans Payable—Furniture, Furnishings, and Equipmer	$	31,341	9.48% $	14,714	3.85%
	FUTA Tax Payable	$	31	0.01% $	32	0.01%
	SUTA Tax Payable	$	40	0.01% $	39	0.01%
	Total Current Liabilities	**$**	**75,686**	**22.90% $**	**128,487**	**33.62%**
Deferred Revenue						
	Deferred Accounts Receivable	$	254,883	77.10% $	253,635	66.38%
	Total Liabilities	**$**	**330,569**	**100.00% $**	**382,122**	**100.00%**
Members' Capital						
	Retained Earnings	$	53,700	11.72% $	50,557	10.52%
	Members' Capital Accounts	$	25,470	5.56% $	57,660	11.99%
	Members' Curr Yr Capital Contrib.	$	1,500	0.33% $	3,613	0.75%
	General Draws	$	(430,445)	-93.94% $	(519,886)	-108.13%
	Draws—Health, Dental	$	(14,574)	-3.18% $	(9,340)	-1.94%
	Draws—Life & Disability Ins.	$	(6,128)	-1.34% $	(3,103)	-0.65%
	Draws—401(K) Deferral	$	(38,093)	-8.31% $	(19,292)	-4.01%
	Current Yr Net Income	$	536,206	117.02% $	538,455	111.99%
	Total Members' Capital	**$**	**127,636**	**27.86% $**	**98,664**	**20.52%**
	Total Liabilities & Capital	**$**	**458,205**	**$**	**480,786**	

36

Things You Need to Do

The Dashboard

Every practice should have a dashboard of financial and performance metrics that the physician leader studies on a regular basis. A good dashboard should include the financial analysis tools that are most important to the organization. Pick which ones you want on the dashboard and use them. Maybe you like a few solvency ratios and some horizontal and vertical analysis. It's completely up to you. Personally, I like the current ratio, working capital, days in A/R, days in A/P, operating margin, and horizontal and vertical analysis for each period. The important thing to do is keep track of your ratios and report them the same way each period. Make it easy to spot trends and changes.

Things You Should Do on a Regular Basis

In medicine, there are certain reports or data we might want or need at different times. If we have a patient on a heparin drip or vancomycin infusion, we might order a PTT or vancomycin level daily or every few hours. If we are treating a diabetic patient, we might check the Hgb-A1C every few months. Different disease states and therapies determine the frequency with which we examine the results.

As you operate your small business, the same principle applies. There are certain reports or data points you might want on a daily, weekly, monthly, or quarterly basis. If you aren't the one looking at these reports, then your assigned delegate should perform these tasks regularly and report the findings to you.

Daily Checks

How much cash do you have in the bank? This should be a daily check for you or someone you delegate this task to (e.g. an office manager or accountant). It's important to understand your receivables and payables, but you use cash to pay your bills today. Knowing your daily cash position is vital for daily operations as well as planning for the future. These are easy things to do on a regular basis. As Jim Rohn said, "Things that are easy to do are easy not to do." It will take discipline, but it's easy enough. So just do it.

Weekly Checks

Who owes you money? How long have they owed you the money? When was the money due? Make certain you, your office staff, or your billing company stays on top of your receivables. Are the claims being worked appropriately? You won't know who hasn't paid you unless you keep track of that information. Don't think just because they owe you money that they'll be nice and pay. Sometimes people need to be reminded of what they owe. A gentle reminder is always helpful.

Whom do you owe money to? When is it due? Can you pay it on time? What is your relationship with those to whom you owe money? Is it possible to renegotiate terms?

After you have determined who owes you money, how much you think you'll get, and whom you plan to pay, you can then project your cash position into the future. This will be very helpful especially if you anticipate needing to utilize a line of credit to make payroll.

Monthly Checks

Review your income statement and balance sheet reports. Compare them to the last month and last year. What changes are you noticing? What seems unexpected? Why did it occur? What seems expected?

Recheck your receivables. Who is late? What is the plan to obtain your money? Where are they in your collection process?

Look at your productivity reports. How did the month go? What do you think will happen next month?

Quarterly Checks

Review your quarterly income statements and balance sheets. What trends are developing over that time? What do you expect to see on the reports?

Examine your productivity reports. Look for any trends. Do they make sense? Does the data you're seeing match with what you're experiencing in the clinic? Try to catch issues as soon as possible.

Annual Checks

Take some time and plan for taxes. Examine your annual income statements, balance sheets, and cash flow statements. Look at how you performed for the entire year. What went well? What improved? What grew? What didn't do so well? What shrank? Why did these changes occur? What's your plan for the next year? Where do you want to be in one year? How will you get there? The annual review is as much, if not more, looking forward as looking back.

PART FOUR

What are Costs?

37

Dr. Collins Gets an Education

Dr. Brian Collins had been practicing medicine for years now. He joined the group right out of residency and enjoyed doing what he loves. His group was mild-mannered until recent years. As reimbursements began to decline and costs escalated, the partners scrutinized their paychecks more and more each month.

Traditionally, the practice had been a "lump-and-dump" practice regarding costs, assignment of insured patients, and revenue. Everyone basically did the same job. No one was particularly proficient in one area or disease. It was your basic bread-and-butter practice.

That all changed a few years ago when they hired a young man to perform endoscopies for their clinic. He was board-certified just like them but obtained additional training in endoscopy. The partners voted and all chipped in to create an endoscopy suite where they could send their patients to their newest and youngest physician.

Everything was fine until they made him a full-fledged partner and he began to look at the books. According to him, something wasn't right. He didn't spend much time in the clinic as he spent two mornings performing scopes. Yet he was being allocated the same overhead as the other physicians who saw patients all day long. He felt his overhead should be less since he used his staff less. Thus began the argument of cost accounting and allocation of overhead.

To prepare for the next board meeting, Dr. Collins asked to meet with a local CPA who managed two other groups in the city.

"Thanks for meeting me, Tom. I really appreciate it," he said as he walked into the conference room.

Tom Castle walked over to shake hands. "Glad to meet you, Dr. Collins. You mentioned in your email you had some questions regarding costs. How may I help you today?" He gestured for him to take a seat.

Dr. Collins explained the situation, history, and issues he saw with the practice. He talked about what he thought was fair and the challenging time he was having trying to get the others to see his side of the story.

Tom took notes, shaking his head, and let Dr. Collins talk. After a while, when Dr. Collins took a breath, Tom asked a few questions.

"That's a common problem among many groups. How exactly are you identifying your fixed costs? How are you tracking your variable costs? What systems are in place to ensure that you accurately capture and allocate your costs?"

"Umm, what's a fixed cost? A variable cost? I'm sorry, but aren't costs just costs?"

"No, there are many types of costs and various ways to track them. Let me start at the beginning and explain the difference between the types of costs. That should give you an idea of how you will want to approach this issue with your partners."

For the next two hours, Tom shared with Dr. Collins the importance of understanding types of costs and how to track costs. This chapter is what Tom shared.

38 | Managerial Accounting

Introduction

Accounting is more than just balance sheets and income statements. It's also tracking the money spent by the firm on goods and services sold. You should have appropriate accounting measures in place to ensure maximum profitability. Tracking costs will become more important in the future as payment structures change. Even though the *how*, *when*, and *why* you get paid will change, your fundamental cost accounting needs will not change.

Why Managerial Accounting?

Managerial accounting is the process of using and tracking information as a business moves toward its goals. This information must be interpreted and communicated properly if it is to be used properly. This particular branch of accounting is sometimes referred to as cost accounting. There are five main processes in which the collected cost information will be used.

Strategy Formulation

The proper strategic decisions can only be made with accurate and precise cost information. With the right information, you can look at the marketplace and determine which services or products would be profitable.

Planning

Good accounting and cost information will help you plan for the future. Managerial decisions such as what is the appropriate point to hire extra personnel or expand services and still be successful are made with cost accounting.

Control

Control is not about absolute dictatorial control as is frequently envisioned when controls measures are discussed. Rather, the old adage "an ounce of prevention is worth a pound of cure" works well in business. Cost controls are not cost cutting measures but rather cost prevention measures. Costs never drift downwards, so cost control is a constant task.

Decision-making

For each and every decision a manager or business owner makes, cost information is imperative to reaching the right—or rather, the best—decision. Whether these decisions involve strategy, planning, or directing, the information about cost must be available to the decision makers.

Directing

Directing and advising others in their duties is only helped with good cost information. If you assign someone the task of improving a process, providing them with good cost data will only help them. They will know where to focus their efforts.

39 | What is a Cost?

A cost is a measure of the value of resources used or consumed by a company to achieve a particular purpose, such as the production of a good or service. It is what we are giving up or spending to provide patient care with the hope of earning a profit. There are many different ways to classify costs.

Types of Costs

Product

Product costs are associated with goods for sale (cost of goods sold, or COGS). All costs that are directly attributable to the COGS are product costs until the time of sale. After that point, these costs become expenses.

Period

Period costs are expensed during the time in which they were incurred. An example would be operating expenses.

Expenses

Expenses represent the consumption of the firm's assets for the purpose of generating revenue.

Manufacturing Costs

Manufacturing costs are all costs involved in the manufacture of a good or service. All labor and materials that are used directly in the production of the good or service are manufacturing costs. Overhead is another type of manufacturing cost.

Direct Material

Direct material cost is the cost of raw material that is used to make a good or service. It can be conveniently traced to a finished product or service. An example would be the steel used to manufacture an automobile. In healthcare, this would be suture for surgery or laboratory blood tubes.

Direct Labor

Direct labor costs are the costs of salaries, wages, and fringe benefits for the personnel who work directly on manufactured products or services. For example, in an automobile plant, the direct labor would be the wages paid to an assembly line worker. For healthcare, it would be the nurse collecting vitals and assisting the physician in the clinic.

Overhead

Overhead is the catchall for the remaining costs. This includes indirect materials, indirect labor, and other costs.

Indirect Materials

Indirect materials are used to support the production process. In an automobile plant, this would be lubricants and cleaning supplies. In healthcare, this might be an electronic medical record program and associated information technology supporting the computers and workstations.

Indirect Labor

Indirect labor is the cost of the personnel who do not work directly on the product. In our plant example, this would be janitorial personnel and security guards. In a healthcare setting, this might be the receptionist and coding personnel.

Other Costs

Other costs include the depreciation on the plant, property, and equipment. Property taxes, insurance, utilities, overtime, and idle time are also reported here.

Cost Classification

The Two Most Important Types of Cost Classification

Not all costs are the same. Some costs change with activity or production and some never go away as long as the firm exists. Knowing what each type of cost is and how it behaves can help the physician know, predict, and ultimately control their costs.

Variable Costs

Variable costs (VC) change when the production activity changes. As the activity increases, the costs of the activity also increase. Figure 4.1 is an example of variable costs. The variable costs per unit produced remain the same over a wide range of activities. It is not necessarily linear in relation, but there is a correlation between the total variable cost and the level of activity. If your variable costs are $10/widget, your costs will increase as you sell more widgets. So, sell 10 widgets, your costs are $100. Sell 20, your costs are $200.

Figure 4.1 - Variable Costs

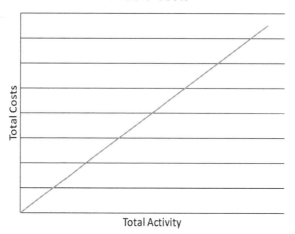

Variable Costs

Employee Wages, Overtime, Benefits
Medical Supplies
Drugs
Transcription Services
Data Processing
Billing and Collection Services Telephone, Postage, and Utilities

Fixed Costs

Fixed costs (FC) do not change when the production activity changes. Figure 4.2 is an example of fixed costs. These costs will not go away as long as the firm exists and works to create a good or service. As the activity of a firm increases, the fixed cost per unit produced will go down, but the cost itself is fixed. As the level of production decreases, the fixed cost per unit produced will go up. Let's say it costs you $1,000/month in rent for your office space. It doesn't matter if you see 100 or 200 patients in a month, your rent is still $1,000. When you see 100 patients, your rent cost per patient is $100, but when you see 200 patients, it becomes $50.

Figure 4.2 - Fixed Costs

Fixed Costs

Total Activity

Employee Salaries
Rent
Equipment Leases
Building and Equipment Maintenance
Property Taxes
Interest on Loans
Legal and Accounting Services
Depreciation

Figure 4.3 shows a summary of the two types of costs we are concerned with in managerial accounting.

Figure 4.3 - Summary of Variable and Fixed Costs

Summary of Variable and Fixed Costs		
Cost	In Total	Per Unit
Variable	Total VC changes as activity level changes	VC per unit remains the same over wide ranges of activity
Fixed	Total FC remains the same even when activity level changes	FC per unit goes down as activity goes up

Other Costs

Controllable and Uncontrollable Costs

Some costs are controllable by the manager or physician while others are not. A cost that can be significantly influenced by a manager is considered a controllable cost. Anything else is considered an uncontrollable cost. The physician should be aware of both but focus on what they and their team can control.

Opportunity Costs

Opportunity costs are the potential benefit that is given up when one alternative is selected over another. The opportunity cost of attending college might be the cost of the tuition plus what you would earn in the marketplace.

Sunk Costs

Sunk costs are all costs incurred in the past, and that cannot be changed by any decisions made now or in the future. Sunk costs should not be considered in the financial decision-making process.

Differential Costs

Differential costs are the costs that differ between alternatives available. For example, you could earn $1,500 per month in your hometown or $2,000 in a nearby city. Your commuting costs are $50 per month in your hometown and $300 per month to the nearby city. Your differential cost would be $250.

Marginal Costs

Marginal costs are the extra costs incurred by the firm to produce one additional unit of goods or services. How much does creating one more automobile or performing one more surgery late at night cost? The answer is your marginal cost for that activity.

Average Costs

Average costs are the total costs to produce a quantity divided by the quantity produced by the firm. Marginal and average costs are functions of both variable and fixed costs.

The Costs and Benefits of Information

Having information is good. However, there can be a point where too much information is a hindrance to the decision-making process. Too much information can impede decision-making and lead to information overload. You will find there is a point when you have enough information to make a good decision. Don't be afraid of making a wrong decision since you can always make another decision to correct that wrong one.

Semi-variable Costs

A semi-variable cost is a cost that is partially fixed and partially variable. The behavior of a semi-variable cost is shown in Figure 4.4. Consider a utility cost. One component of this cost is fixed. In a clinic, electricity will always be used to power the security systems, computers, and other essential items. Now let's say the clinic decides to extend their hours of operation by two hours each day. The variable component of this cost will be evident as the lights are on longer—the costs rise higher.

Figure 4.4 - Semi-variable Costs

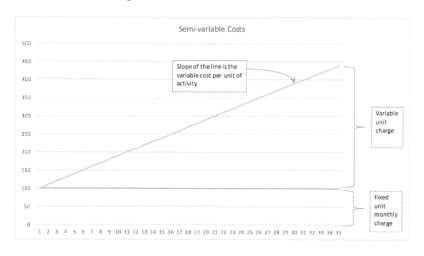

The horizontal line represents your fixed monthly costs. You begin to use the service—your costs increase. The best example I can think of for a semi-variable cost is your cellular data plan. You probably pay $100 for 5GB of data each month. If you don't use all your data, you still pay $100. However, the minute your kids stream YouTube videos of cats running from cucumbers, your data consumption goes over 5GB, and then your variable costs go into effect.

Cost of Quality

Quality can cost the firm money in a number of ways. There are prevention costs, internal failure costs, and external failure costs. A practice must constantly focus on the quality of their products and services.

Prevention costs are incurred because you are trying to keep bad things from happening. Bad things can range from being late in your day to a patient expiring. What is the cost of preventing something bad from happening? For example, what is the cost of having two nurses confirm the drug that is about to be given?

Internal failure costs are those your practice incurs. They only affect the practice and those within it. Let's say, for instance, that your phone system goes down, or your EMR fails. What are the costs to your practice if that happens?

External failure costs are those costs incurred by those outside your practice. Medical malpractice enters into the picture here. Hopefully, you won't have to deal with or worry about those costs because you've got systems and people in place that prevent harm from coming to your patient.

Even though prevention costs can be high, failure costs can also be expensive, particularly those that occur with the customer. The opportunity cost of lost sales and decreased market share can represent a significant hidden cost to the firm.

Customer Profitability Analysis

Part of cost accounting is understanding what it costs you to provide your goods or services to a particular customer. It's important to remember that not every customer is a good customer. If you examine your cost and profitability information for each customer or carrier type, you can gain some valuable insight. It can help you know where to focus on which customers you should be trying to attract and retain. You can also see the effects of your discounting decisions.

Sometimes customers, patients, and insurance companies can be bad for a practice. Always consider those who ask for special items or services, large discounts, fast responses, or change their requests frequently to be questionable customers. Some payers might not be worth your time and energy. They may want discounts that are too steep for your practice.

Don't be afraid to say no. Don't feel guilty about turning away patients you will lose money on. It's not your patients' fault they have a bad payer, but you cannot keep your doors open if you are losing money each month. You help those whom you can help.

40 | Cost Estimation

Cost estimation is the process of determining cost behavior. Typically, we use historical data to arrive at our conclusions. You get this information from your accountant and the reports they generate. The first step is to look at the historical costs. Once you have those numbers, you can try to establish what the relationship is between the cost and the activity that generated the cost. Finally, you create a model and attempt to predict costs. This is important as you create budgets and projections. Later, I'll give you an example of how this might be accomplished.

Cost Estimation Methods

Estimating costs is critical for any business, practice, or government unit. Being able to reliably and accurately predict the future costs is important as you begin to create a budget for future fiscal periods. Fortunately, there are some tools available to assist the physician in peering into the future.

Account Classification

With the account classification method, cost estimates are based on a review of each account making up the total cost being analyzed. Each item on the report is examined and averaged over the time period and then projected forward with the appropriate growth rates. This is an excellent method if you have your accounting system set up for it.

However, elaborate accounting systems cost money. You will need to determine how much you are willing to spend to obtain your cost information. You and your accountant will need to sit down and discuss how you want to classify your costs and how they will be tracked. Break out a big pot of coffee and pen and paper and get to work with them. But once you're done, it should be easier to collect and analyze cost data.

Visual Fit

The visual fit method is very simple to use. You collect all of your cost data for given periods. You will also need the corresponding activity data for those periods. Then you can graph the data points on a chart. Plot costs as a function of the activity and you will wind up with a scatter plot of your cost data. Next, you draw a line that best fits your data points. This becomes your cost equation. You can easily do this with Excel or another spreadsheet program. An example is shown in Figure 4.5.

Figure 4.5 - Visual Fit Method

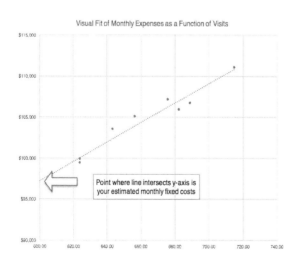

This method can be helpful in analyzing the mixed costs of the firm. The fixed costs are the point where the line intersects with the y-axis. The slope of the line gives you an estimate of your variable costs. This can be helpful in budgeting and projecting into the future.

Least Squares Regression

This is a statistical process used to determine the relationship between variables such as activity and cost. The objective of the regression method is to create a general cost equation. Using the equation below, we can predict the cost of future periods.

$$Y = a + bX$$

In this equation, Y is the total cost and the dependent variable. The intercept term a is the estimated fixed costs. X is the activity level and is the independent variable. The variable cost coefficient is b. We can use tools such as spreadsheets (Excel) or other statistical programs to determine this equation. In Excel or Numbers, under the chart options, there is an option to display the equation of the line using a variety of different methods, such as linear, exponential, etc. An example is shown in Figure 4.6.

If you would like to learn more, there are excellent websites that provide more detail on the application of this method. You can find help at support.microsoft.com, wikihow.com, excel-easy.com, and youtube.com.

Figure 4.6 - Regression Model

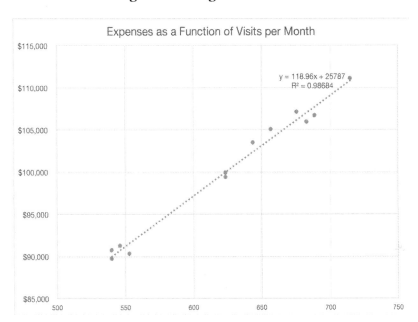

Data Collection Issues

The models generated using these methods are only as good as the data used in their calculations. The physician must keep in mind what data are missing. They must decide how to handle the outliers. They must also make sure that time period costs are properly matched to the activities. Tradeoffs will also be made when determining which time periods to use. The physician not only needs to know how to use the data, but they must also know if their data is good and how bad data might impact their final conclusions.

41

The Break-even Point

The break-even point is a must-know if you plan to run any business successfully. It is the point where the volume of activity makes the firm's revenues and expenses equal. Profit is not made, but money is not lost either. Determining this point is critical when analyzing new products or services. There are a couple of different approaches to determine the break-even point.

The Equation Approach

The equation approach is simple and relatively straightforward. To utilize this method, you must have a few bits of information. First, you must know what your revenues are. This can be real or projected. Next, you need to know what your variable costs are. As we discussed earlier, variable costs follow activity level but typically stay constant over a wide range of activity levels. Finally, we need to know our fixed costs. Then we can set up the equation like this:

$$\text{Revenue - Variable costs - Fixed costs} = \text{Profit}$$

In our example, we assume Physicians of America will have collections of $500 per patient visit. From their analysis, they've determined their variable costs to be $300 per patient visit. They know their fixed costs are around $80,000 per month. They've used the previously discussed cost estimation methods to find that their contribution margin is about $200 per patient visit. If we set our equation equal to zero (that is, our profit is zero), we can solve it for our break-even point of patient visits needed per month:

Revenue - Variable Costs - Fixed = Profit

($500 x patient visits) - ($300 x patient visits) - $80,000 = 0

$200 x patient visits = $80,000

Patient visits = 400

POA needs to see about 400 patients each month if they are to break even. If they see fewer than 400 patients, they will dip into the red and lose money.

Although the equation method is simple, we might consider using the contribution margin approach. It's a little more advanced in its approach to finding the break-even point.

Contribution Margin

Contribution margin (CM) is how much of each dollar of revenue goes to covering the fixed costs of the business. A contribution margin of 10% means that for every $1 in revenue, $0.10 goes to covering the fixed costs of the business. Mathematically, it would look like this:

Contribution Margin = Price - Variable Costs

If POA collects $500 per patient visit and it costs them $300 per patient visit in variable costs, their contribution margin is $200 per patient visit. For each patient they see, $200 (40% of the collected fee) goes to cover the fixed costs of the clinic.

Contribution Margin Approach

This method uses revenue instead of units of activity needed. We want to see how much revenue POA needs to break even every month. For this method, we need the contribution margin and the fixed costs.

$$\text{Break-even Revenue} = \frac{\text{Fixed Costs}}{\text{Contribution Margin}}$$

It's been determined that POA's fixed costs are about $80,000 per month. We have also determined that the contribution margin is about $200 per patient visit; 40% of collections goes to cover the fixed costs.

$$\text{Break-even Revenue} = \frac{\text{Fixed Costs}}{\text{Contribution Margin}}$$

$$\text{Break-even Revenue} = \frac{\$80,000}{40\%} = \$200,000$$

Solving for the break-even revenue, we discover that POA needs about $200,000 in revenue each month to break even. From there, we can also verify the number of visits needed. At $500/visit, we again find POA needs 400 visits each month.

This method allows the practice to determine how much a product or service contributes to the fixed expenses of the practice. This data is very important when examining product or services lines and whether it is a proper decision to close or discontinue a line or not.

Cost-Volume-Profit Graph

With the cost-volume-profit graph method, total sales and total expenses are plotted as a function of units. The point where these two lines cross represents the break-even volume and sales dollars. This is illustrated in Figure 4.7.

Figure 4.7 – Cost-Volume-Profit Graph

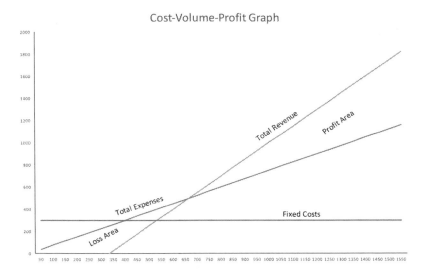

Cost-Volume-Profit Graph

This graph is easy to create. You simply plot your revenue graph against your expense graph. This can be done in Excel or any other spreadsheet.

Target Net Profit

It is possible to determine the number of units needed to sell in order to earn a particular desired profit. This time we are solving for the patient visits needed to generate a desired monthly profit. In this case, they want $100,000 of profit each month. We set up the equation like this:

$$\text{Units Needed to Generate Target Profit} = \frac{\text{Fixed Costs} + \text{Target Profit}}{\text{Patient Visit Contribution Margin}}$$

After we plug the numbers into the equation, we find POA needs to see about 900 patients every month to generate a profit of

$100,000 each month. That's twice what they are currently doing. The next question is this, "Is that reasonable and possible?"

$$\text{Units Needed to Generate Target Profit} = \frac{\text{Fixed Costs} + \text{Target Profit}}{\text{Patient Visit Contribution Margin}}$$

$$\text{Units Needed to Generate Target Profit} = \frac{\$80,000 + \$100,000}{\$200/\text{patient visit}} = 900 \text{ patient visits}$$

Safety Margin

Safety margin is an important concept. It is the difference between the budgeted revenue and the break-even revenue. It's the number by which activity can drop before a loss is incurred by the practice. For POA, their break-even point is $200,000 or 400 patients. Currently, they see about 500 patients each month. So they have a safety margin of $50,000 or 100 patients. This is why knowing your costs, revenues, and volumes each month is important. If you monitor these items, you will be able to see negative trends and take action sooner rather than later.

Changes in Fixed Costs

Fixed costs can be a drain on your cash and revenue if you're not careful. Before taking on any new endeavor, it's important to evaluate the financial impact of the costs and revenue of the endeavor.

Let's say one of POA's partner's brother-in-law is a salesman for an internet marketing firm. He claims that for just $10,000 per month, they should be able to bring an additional 40 patients into the clinic. That's an additional revenue of $20,000 per month. That's an impressive return on the investment, or so claims the sales guy. Let's take a closer look at this scenario beginning with the current state in Figure 4.8.

Figure 4.8 - Current State Analysis

	Current
Visits	500
Revenue	$ 250,000
Less VC	$ 150,000
Contribution margin	$ 100,000
Less FC	$ 80,000
Net income	$ 20,000

POA is currently seeing about 500 patients each month. They see about $20,000 in monthly profit. For a mere $10,000 each month, they are told they can push their profit to $40,000 each month. However, one partner is wary and decides to run the numbers. What he discovers is shown in Figure 4.9.

Figure 4.9 - Proposed State

	Current	Proposed
Visits	500	540
Revenue	$250,000	$270,000
Less VC	$150,000	$162,000
Contribution margin	$100,000	$108,000
Less FC	$ 80,000	$ 90,000
Net income	$ 20,000	$ 18,000

Yes, the revenue of the clinic will increase by $20,000. However, the variable costs will also rise with the increased activity level. The contribution margin only grows by $8,000. Hmmm, not looking too good at this point. What happens to the fixed costs? Well, they increase by $10,000 which is the cost of the internet marketing firm. At the end of the day, the net profit will only be $18,000. That means that the $10,000 internet marketing cost will not pay for itself and will also cost the practice $2,000 in monthly profit.

Two lessons can be learned here. First, always, always, *always* run your numbers. Second, don't ever trust the numbers given to you by any sales representative, even if they are family or a friend.

42 | Cost Accounting Ratios

Here are a couple of managerial accounting ratios to watch for:

- People ratios
- Non-medical staff/provider ratios

Every practice will have office personnel to assist with the operation of the practice. Secretaries, coders, transcriptionists, and office managers are all necessary for a functional clinic.

Total Staffing per Provider

This would include all the staff, clinical and non-clinical. It's a measure of how many people each healthcare provider uses.

Productivity Ratios

No-shows per Provider per Time Period

Knowing this information is valuable for schedulers as they plan a physician's day. If this number gets larger, investigate the reason. Who is the typical no-show patient? Can you overbook the day to accommodate the no-shows and maintain a productive day?

Visits per Provider per Day

Look at how many patients each provider sees each day. How long does each provider see each patient? How does the severity or complexity of their patients affect this ratio?

Physician Cancelation Rate

It's rare, but sometimes physicians must cancel their appointments. It's usually because the physician is ill or they are running behind schedule and will not be able to catch up for the day. Sometimes physicians must cancel due to unforeseen or unplanned emergencies (this is more common with procedural or surgical specialists).

Track and monitor the rate at which providers cancel. Look for patterns and attempt to alter the scheduling to accommodate for such instances if they occur frequently. Also, with this data, you will be able to warn the patients when they schedule their appointment that there is a chance the physician will run late. Try to set the patients' expectations early in the relationship.

No-show to Appointment Ratio

What is your no-show rate? Who typically fails to show up for their appointment? Is there a particular patient population or individual patient who does this frequently? This information can be used to safeguard your schedule. You will also know which patients you need to remind more frequently about their appointments.

Patient Cancelation Rate

This is similar to the no-show rate, except these patients are courteous enough to let you know they won't be showing up. It might be helpful to learn why patients are canceling their appointments so you can work to prevent it from happening in the future.

Performance Ratios

Marketing Costs per New Patient

Look at how well marketing expenditures are generating new patients for the physician. What can boost the marketing's effectiveness? What is the physician's reputation? How can you get this image out to the public?

Occupancy Expenses per Provider

This is an overhead cost ratio. These are the costs of occupying a space. It includes rent, taxes, insurance, depreciation and amortization costs. Is this ratio increasing or decreasing?

Average Revenue per Patient

This is the average revenue per patient per given period of time. It is useful for budgeting and forecasting. What does the trend show? Why is it going up, down, or remaining level?

Average Revenue per Encounter

Another useful forecasting, budgeting, and performance ratio is the average revenue per encounter. This is an important ratio to follow if your practice provides ancillary services such as radiology, laboratory, etc.

Average Cost per Patient

This is an important metric to follow. Look for ways to keep it as low as possible. This information will be helpful as you plan for the future.

Profitability Ratios

Collection Ratio

The collection ratio measures the consequences of negotiated contracts against the organization's overall earnings. How much are you collecting compared to what you charge? What are your anticipated collections? How close are your actual collections to that number? If there is a variance between them, ask why and try to find the problem. After you do that, you'll be able to implement a solution.

Days in A/R

Days in A/R shows how long it takes the practice to collect the money it is owed for services rendered. This number should be as low as possible. If the number gets too big, then the practice could face cash flow issues. If a change in the ratio is observed, especially if it grows larger, then you should investigate. Look for explanations for the change. Has something happened to the coding and billing process? Who is contributing to the rise the most? Which payers seem to be paying later?

RVUs

RVUs

Relative value units (RVUs) are a unique method of measuring and reporting productivity in a clinic setting. They are numeric values placed upon the reimbursement assigned to specific services provided by the physician.

Each CPT code has an RVU assigned to it. Then the RVU is multiplied by a conversion factor (CF) and a geographical adjustment factor (GPCI) to create the compensation level for the specific service provided. RVUs aren't difficult to calculate. There are many resources on the web that you can use to figure it out. What is important is to know what your basic, most common visits and procedures generate in terms of RVUs. This will be particularly important if you are negotiating or getting paid for the RVUs you generate.

PART FIVE

Financing

43 | Does It Make Sense?

Dr. Blake Carr hung up the phone. The sales representative made some good points. Blake expected him to do that because it was his job to sell. However, a new ultrasound machine would be nice. They could use it to provide point-of-care testing. They would have the results immediately. It could make things a lot better for the patients. But did it make sense financially? Was this the best place to spend their money? Were there other places or assets that would be better to invest in?

Dr. Carr decided to open his laptop and use his trusty spreadsheet to find the answers to these questions.

In this section, you will be introduced to the concepts used in capital expenditure planning. You will learn the concept of the time value of money and how it is used to make investment decisions. You will learn what the hurdle rate is and how it is used. We will examine present value, future value, and net present value.

The goal of this section is to make you more aware of how investment decisions are made. This information will also be important to you if you work in large organizations that have large capital expenditure budgets.

44

The Time Value of Money

The time value of money (TMV) is an incredibly important and fundamental concept to understand when you are making financial decisions. Whether it's in your personal life or business life, comprehending and applying the concept of TVM will help guide you to make strong, solid financial decisions.

The concept is simple, and we all understand it. A dollar today buys more than a dollar will tomorrow, or in one year, or ten years. The purchasing power of a dollar continues to dwindle over time. Knowing that, we have a few tools that will help us make the best investments with today's dollars. Use your dollars now to maximize their value or return for tomorrow. That's what we will be discussing in the following pages. I will provide you an introduction to some of the key concepts in financial decision-making. You will learn to use valuable tools that will assist you in making capital expenditure decisions as well as understanding why others (hospitals, clinics, surgery centers) make the decisions they do.

Future Value

Since we understand the time value of money—today's dollars buy more than tomorrow's dollars—let's look at the *future value*. Future value (FV) is the value a given amount of cash will be worth in the future at a specific time. If we want to know what a dollar will be worth tomorrow, we use future value.

The equation for finding the future value of an investment is pretty simple and straightforward.

Future value = Present value * (1 + Rate of return)$^{\text{Number of periods investment is held}}$

$$FV = PV * (1 + r)^n$$

FV represents the future value. PV is the present value of the investment. The rate is represented by r and the number of periods the investment is held is n. If you buy a bank certificate of deposit (CD), this is the equation you would use to see how much money you will have when the CD matures.

One of the most important and yet difficult points in this calculation is picking the right interest rate. How conservative do you need to be? What assumptions are you making or using in building your models? Pick a number too high, and the result might make you too optimistic. Pick too low a number, and the result might make you too pessimistic and pass on a deal.

Let's look at an example. You've been offered an investment that will pay you 5% each year. It costs $10,000 to acquire the investment. In three years, how much will your investment be?

$$FV = PV * (1 + r)^n = \$10,000 * (1 + 0.05)^3 = \$11,576.25$$

In three years, your $10,000 investment would be worth $11,576.25 if it grew at 5%. Again, this is the same calculation you will use whether you're dealing with CDs, savings accounts, whole life insurance, or the purchase of an asset.

When we consider capital investments in our practice, one of the most important tasks is determining which assumptions you should make. Is a 3% growth rate appropriate? Perhaps a 6% is more realistic. What if everything was perfect and we saw a 9% growth? The model you build is only as solid as the assumptions you make. Be very careful and mindful of the assumptions you're making when evaluating investments. These projects can be fun to think about. However, we must keep a strong dose of reality when reviewing these projections.

Present Value

Present value (PV) is the same equation we just looked at but rearranged to solve for PV instead of FV. In the lexicon of the financial world, interest rates move forward, and discount rates move backward. PV is used most frequently for capital expenditures. It moves the value of money backward in time and lets you see what tomorrow's dollars are worth today.

Let's say you've got a piece of fancy equipment you want to purchase and think it'll generate $10,000 in annual revenue over its useful life of three years. What's it worth? Or said another way, how much should you spend to acquire the asset? This is where PV comes into the picture.

To make investment decisions, you must make two assumptions. First, you must assume what the revenue will be. Second, you must determine what growth rate you might get somewhere else or in another investment. Once you have those two numbers, you can perform the calculation.

Look at the equation for present value below. *PV* is the present value. *FV* is our future value. Our interest rate is *r* and our number of periods is *n*. Typically *n* is in years, but you can use any period, especially if the interest compounds.

$$\text{Present value} = \frac{\text{Future value}}{(1 + \text{Rate of return})^{\text{number of periods investment is held}}}$$

$$PV = \frac{FV}{(1+r)^n}$$

Back to our example: you have been offered an investment which will pay you $10,000 in three years. If you can put your money in a certificate of deposit at your bank where you'll earn 2% per year, what should you pay today for $10,000 in three years?

$$PV = \frac{FV}{(1+r)^n} = \frac{\$10,000}{(1+0.02)^3} = \$9,423.22$$

According to this calculation, if you want $10,000 in three years and earn 2%, then you should pay no more than $9,423.22. What happens if we change the interest?

$$PV = \frac{FV}{(1+r)^n} = \frac{\$10,000}{(1+0.05)^3} = \$8,638.38$$

At a 5% return, you would pay no more than $8,638.38. What does a 10% return look like?

$$PV = \frac{FV}{(1+r)^n} = \frac{\$10,000}{(1+0.10)^3} = \$7,513.15$$

You would pay no more than $7,513.15 to get a 10% return on your money over the next three years. If you are considering the purchase of equipment or an asset, you will use a similar calculation to determine what the value of the asset is today.

Know What Your Capital Costs You

As we have examined earlier in this book, there are two ways to finance your practice or business. First, you can use loans and borrow the money. We all know most loans come with an interest rate and we will pay back more than we borrowed. That's the cost of borrowing the capital you need. Another way to finance your business is to sell ownership, to give equity in exchange for capital. When you purchase stock in a company, as an investor you expect a return on your money. When you sell someone equity, they too will expect a return.

When we have both loans and equity as methods of capital, then we need to discover what our real cost of capital is going to be. This is also called our hurdle rate. We have two mouths to feed, if you will. If we don't bring in enough food to feed both of them, we can get into trouble. So we want to look for opportunities that will at a minimum feed both our lenders and shareholders. This is the hurdle we must clear when investing the capital of the business or practice.

Cost of Capital

In trying to determine your hurdle rate, a couple of pieces of information are necessary. First, you need to know the financial structure of your company. What is the debt to equity ratio? Next, you will need to know the cost of each type of financing. What do you pay for your loans? What return do your investors expect to earn? Armed with this information, you can calculate your hurdle rate using the following equation.

Cost of capital = (% Debt on the books)*(Cost of the debt)+(% of equity on the books)*(Cost of the equity)

Let's assume you have a debt to equity ratio of 0.25. You are currently paying 5% on your loans, and your investors expect a return on their capital of 12%. Your hurdle rate would look like this.

Cost of capital = (25%)*(5%)+(75%)*(12%) = 10%

According to this calculation, you would need to earn at least 10% on any investment you make. This way you can be certain you cover your loans, your investors are given their expected returns, and hopefully, everyone is happy.

The Hurdle Rate

The required hurdle rate, or return on investment, will be very important as you try to determine what the PV of your opportunity really is. Making the correct assumption can have a huge impact on the financial outcome of your capital investments.

Let's look at how this all works. Physicians of America wants to buy a fancy new piece of equipment to use in their clinic. They have done the analysis and believe it will generate $100,000 in annual revenue over the course of its useful life, four years.

Since our discussion of TVM has shown that money received tomorrow isn't worth as much as money received today, POA needs to account for that in their decision-making process. The basic question begins with "what return is reasonable?" If they invested money in the market today, what return would they likely get?

It is best to be conservative and realistic in answering this question. If you wanted $100,000 one year from now, how much should you invest? It really depends on the interest rate you will get. In your checking account, you might earn 2% so you would need to plunk down $98,039 to have $100,000 in one year. Let's say you wanted $100,000 four years from now. If you have a rate of 2% and let the money sit for four years, you would need to put down $92,385 to have $100,000 in four years. Again, present value is just the opposite of future value.

When deciding capital expenditures, you would typically start with a discounted cash flow analysis. This begins with the present value of the revenue for each period of time you are using. In our example, the machine will generate $100,000 in revenue each year for a total of $400,000 in total revenue. Remember, the revenue it creates in Year 1 is more valuable than the revenue in Year 4 because Year 1 is closer to the present than Year 4. We can create a table to show the value of the revenue for each year, with each progressive year being worth less than the prior year.

To determine the total value of the cash flow, we simply add up all the years. Looking at the table below, we see a variety of rates listed. At a 2% return rate, we have a value of cash flow of $380,773. That means that if POA wanted $400,000 in four years, they should spend $380,773 in today's dollars. As we go down the table, we see the powerful effect of the rate they decide to use. Using a 10% return rate, they should spend $316,987. Spending more than $316,987 will not clear their hurdle rate. If they did purchase the equipment for more, they would receive less than a 10% return on their investment. However, if they can secure the equipment for $300,000, then their return will increase and be higher than their hurdle rate of 10%. An analysis of the cash flows for each different rate of return is shown in Figure 5.1.

Figure 5.1 - Analysis of Cash Flows

Year

Rate	1	2	3	4	PV of Cash Flows
2%	$ 98,039	$ 96,117	$ 94,232	$ 92,385	$ 380,773
4%	$ 96,154	$ 92,456	$ 88,900	$ 85,480	$ 362,990
6%	$ 94,340	$ 89,000	$ 83,962	$ 79,209	$ 346,511
8%	$ 92,593	$ 85,734	$ 79,383	$ 73,503	$ 331,213
10%	$ 90,909	$ 82,645	$ 75,131	$ 68,301	$ 316,987
15%	$ 86,957	$ 75,614	$ 65,752	$ 57,175	$ 285,498
20%	$ 83,333	$ 69,444	$ 57,870	$ 48,225	$ 258,873

45 | It Costs Money to Make Money: Figuring out Capital Expenditures

You've heard it said many times before: it takes money to make money. Well, that is very true. As we have discussed, it takes money to purchase assets that are used to generate revenue. How we get that money depends on our preferences. Do we raise capital by selling equity and ownership, or do we borrow it? That part is important, but what's more important is figuring out if purchasing a particular asset will be worth it in the end.

In this chapter, we will examine a few different methods for determining the value of an investment. We have examined present value, future value, and discounted cash flow to help us determine the value of an investment. Next, let's look at a few other methods to give us a better picture of the situation.

Capital Expenditures

Capital expenditures are large purchases a company makes. Other words you might hear in the financial lexicon are CapEx, capital investments, and capital budgeting. The bottom line is that someone sat down, looked at the asset, and made some assumptions about its revenue and costs. Then they performed an analysis using the hurdle rate of the company to determine if the investment was worth the company's capital or not.

For example, Physicians of America wants to buy a new CT machine for their main office clinic. These things don't seem to be getting any cheaper with time. It's also going to take quite a bit of cash. Now, the CT company has some nice financing offers, so let's take a look at the process.

First, they need to determine how much cash they need to put into the deal. Sometimes this is referred to as cash outlay. It's just like buying a car or home: you put down cash to acquire the asset. You can pay cash for the entire cost if you want. However, would you be better off using some of that cash in a different area or on a different asset? You won't know until you analyze.

So, back to our initial cost assumptions. What POA puts down is probably only part of the cash outlay. What other costs might be associated with this purchase? Training costs? Installation costs? If they already have an older CT scanner, how long will it take to remove the old one and install the new one? What revenue will be lost during the installation time? If they don't have a scanner, where would they put it? Do they need to add on to the building? What are those costs?

As you can see, there will be many questions you will want to ask as you build your own plan. Try to have cost data that is as accurate as possible, and be conservative (if not a little pessimistic) in your approach. You want to use the capital in a responsible manner.

The next step is for POA to project the future cash flow or revenues from the asset (this is an educated guess, mind you). This is also tricky and can become clouded by rosy, blue sky, and rainbow thinking if one isn't careful. It's best to use the conservatism principle and err on the side of caution.

Finally, POA must look at each of the cash flows from each period and figure out the return on investment. Does the ROI meet their hurdle rate? If so, by how much? Should they buy it? To determine this, we will use payback period, the net present value (NPV), and the internal rate of return (IRR).

Payback Period

This is the simplest way to determine if you should proceed with the purchase of an asset. This formula shows how many years or revenue periods it will take for you to make back your initial investment. It is very easy to calculate this number. You can quickly see if the payback period is longer or shorter than the life of the asset or project. If the asset only lasts 10 years and it takes 11 to get your money back, then you probably should avoid that asset.

We simply take the cash outlay and divide it by the revenue of the period of time we are using. If you buy an asset for $150,000 and it generates revenue of $100,000 per year, your payback period is 1.5 years.

$$\text{Payback period} = \frac{\text{Cash outlay}}{\text{Revenue of the period}}$$

$$\text{Payback period} = \frac{\$150,000}{\$100,000} = 1.5 \text{ years}$$

$$\text{Payback period} = \frac{\$300,000}{\$100,000} = 3 \text{ years}$$

Easy is nice, but it isn't always best. Many times the easy way leaves some important things out. It tells you how long you must hold the asset until you break even, but it doesn't do much other than that. It also doesn't consider the revenue beyond the payback period. It doesn't consider the TVM in the calculation. A dollar can lose quite a bit of power over time, especially a decade.

Payback period is good if you're comparing assets, but not if you're deciding to accept or reject assets. It a good rule of thumb, but that's really about it. Don't hang your hat on it. Use it as a comparison tool.

Net Present Value

NPV is a more complex method of evaluating an asset. It's powerful and takes longer to do, but will give you a better idea of where you will be with the asset at the end of the deal.

NPV is strong because it does take into consideration the time value of money. It also uses your hurdle rate in the evaluation and gives a value in today's dollars with regards to the real value of the asset.

We have already learned how to calculate the present value of an investment. To find the NPV, we calculate the present value for each period the investment is held and add them all together. Next, we subtract the initial cash outlay from the sum total of the PVs. The number we get is the NPV for the asset.

$$\sum_{n=1}^{N} PV$$

$$\sum_{n=1}^{N} PV = \frac{FV}{(1+r)} + \frac{FV}{(1+r)^2} + \frac{FV}{(1+r)^3} \dots + \dots \frac{FV}{(1+r)^n}$$

$$PV = \frac{\$100{,}000}{(1+0.15)} + \frac{\$100{,}000}{(1+0.15)^2} + \frac{\$100{,}000}{(1+0.15)^3} \dots + \dots \frac{\$100{,}000}{(1+0.15)^{10}} = \$501{,}877$$

$$NPV = \$501{,}877 - \$300{,}000 = \$201{,}877$$

In our example, the scanner generates $100,000 in annual revenue for ten years, and POA put $300,000 in cash down to acquire the asset. We determined the hurdle rate to be 15%. They have some higher interest loans and the shareholders have been wanting a stronger return on their investments. After crunching the numbers, we find the NPV to be $201,877. Excellent! The company will earn $201,877 over the course of ten years by acquiring this CT scanner. The results of this analysis are shown in Figure 5.2.

Figure 5.2 - NPV Analysis

Rate	1	2	3	4	10	PV of Cash Flows	Cash Outlay	NPV
2%	$ 98,039	$ 96,117	$ 94,232	$ 92,385	$ 82,035	$ 898,259	$ 300,000	$ 598,259
4%	$ 96,154	$ 92,456	$ .88,900	$ 85,480	$ 67,556	$ 811,090	$ 300,000	$ 511,090
6%	$ 94,340	$ 89,000	$ 83,962	$ 79,209	$ 55,839	$ 736,009	$ 300,000	$ 436,009
8%	$ 92,593	$ 85,734	$ 79,383	$ 73,503	$ 46,319	$ 671,008	$ 300,000	$ 371,008
10%	$ 90,909	$ 82,645	$ 75,131	$ 68,301	$ 38,554	$ 614,457	$ 300,000	$ 314,457
15%	$ 86,957	$ 75,614	$ 65,752	$ 57,175	$ 24,718	$ 501,877	$ 300,000	$ 201,877
20%	$ 83,333	$ 69,444	$ 57,870	$ 48,225	$ 16,151	$ 419,247	$ 300,000	$ 119,247

Unfortunately, that isn't exactly true.

If NPV is greater than 0, you've cleared your hurdle rate and the asset should yield a return on investment greater than your hurdle rate. An important thing to keep in mind is that as your hurdle rate climbs, your NPV decreases. Even if your hurdle rate is 20%, the analysis shows the NPV is still positive, and you would be safe proceeding with the acquisition of the asset.

The important thing to keep in mind is that you'd be safe if all of your assumptions about the revenue and costs of the CT over the course of ten years are accurate. If your revenue drops (say, CMS cuts the reimbursement for CT scans in half), or the costs of maintaining the CT scanner rise above your assumptions, the whole deal changes. NPV is just one of the methods we use. The final method is the internal rate of return.

Internal Rate of Return

The internal rate of return is a bit different from NPV in that you're calculating or solving for an interest rate or the return rate. When we calculate the internal rate of return, we want to find what the return rate of the cash flow is when we set NPV equal to zero. We are solving for the rate, r, when NPV is zero. Then, we compare this calculated rate to the hurdle rate. If your hurdle rate is less than the calculated internal rate of return, then the acquisition of the asset will likely be profitable. If the hurdle rate is greater than the internal rate of return, you might want to look at other investment opportunities.

In our example, POA is laying out $300,000 in cash for the CT scanner. Using the discounted cash flow, we find the NPV of the CT scanner. We can then work backward to discover the internal rate of return. The calculated internal rate of return at the end of ten years would be 31%. It's definitely above their hurdle rate. This calculation is more complex and usually done with financial tools. A sample of a report is shown in Figure 5.3 The math is complex and only fun if you enjoy that sort of stuff.

Figure 5.3 - Internal Rate of Return

	Years					
	0	1	2	3	4	10
Cash flow	$ (300,000)	$ 100,000	$ 100,000	$ 100,000	$ 100,000	$ 100,000
IRR		-67%	-23%	0%	13%	31%

Any financial calculator or Excel can quickly make the calculation for you. Another method you can use is to figure out where the NPV might equal zero. Since we know NPV goes down as the rate increases, we can play with the rate in a table and continue to solve for the different Net Present Value as we change the rate. I would recommend using a financial calculator, Excel, or another spreadsheet program, or any number of various websites that will calculate the number for you. It's not hard to plug the numbers in and click a button.

Our Brand New CT Scanner

So, should POA buy the scanner or not? $300,000 is a lot of cash to plunk down on an asset. However, it appears it would be a strong acquisition for POA. The payback period is three years, which is less than the life of the asset. The Net Present Value is positive at their hurdle rate of 15%. The internal rate of return over ten years is 31%, which also beats their hurdle rate. All the analysis points to the purchase of a new CT scanner, and it should be profitable—assuming the assumptions used to build the model are accurate to begin with.

PART SIX

Real-world Examples

46

Step by Step Guides

I like systems and checklists. Since I'm a pilot, they make a lot of sense to me. Checklists help me avoid missing things as I get a plane ready to fly. I take a similar approach when I examine financial reports. I have assembled my basic checklists that I use when I examine financial reports. I use these so that I don't miss something important. Many people will rush to the bottom line, but I've found that the details and important information are in what's above the bottom line. Take time and force yourself to look above the line because that is what leads to the bottom line.

Step by Step Guide to Reading Income Statements

The Very First Step!

The first and most important step in reading income statements and balance sheets is to make certain you actually have both of these reports from your accountant. If you don't, ask for them. In fact, demand them. Each report is just one-half of the picture.

Income Statement Analysis

Step 1

Look at the date at the top of the page. What period does this report cover? How many clinical days were in the period? Is this a final report or an estimate?

Step 2

Examine the revenue of the period. Where did you make money? What services brought in the most cash? What services brought in the least? What were the largest and smallest contributors to the revenue? What were the contractual write-offs? What was the amount of bad debt? What was your patient volume for this period? It's handy to have operational data to go along with the income statement because that will help you understand your costs and revenue based upon the activity for the period.

Step 3

What's the net revenue for the report? Does it agree with your previous projections? Does it make sense when you consider the associated patient volume?

Step 4

How does this period compare to the last period? What might explain any changes? What changes did you make that might be seen on this report?

Step 5

Examine the costs/expenses. Are there any surprises? What was your biggest cost? Why?

Step 6

How do these costs compare to previous periods? How are your costs trending? What was the associated activity for this period? What was the patient volume for this period and previous periods?

Step 7

Look at the bottom line. Is it growing? Is it stable? What's the trend? Has it met your projections? What might explain what you see?

Step by Step Guide to Reading Balance Sheets

Balance Sheet Analysis

Step 1

Look at the date at the top of the page. How does it relate to the income statement? Hopefully, it is the same date as the last day of the period of time on the income statement.

Step 2

Examine the assets. How much cash do you have? What are your current assets? What are your long-term assets? What are your largest assets? What are your total assets?

Step 3

Compare the assets to previous reports. How have your assets changed? How has your cash position changed? Why has it changed? What did you expect it to be? Why might it be different?

Step 4

Look at the liabilities. What are your current liabilities? When are they due? What are your long-term liabilities? What is your largest liability? What's your total debt?

Step 5

How have your liabilities changed compared to previous reports? Is your debt growing or shrinking? Which type of liability is changing: current or long-term? Do you know why your liabilities are growing? Do you have a plan to control your liabilities?

Step 6

Examine the equity. Is your equity growing or contracting? Why? What have your distributions been doing? Are you going to need to ask for a contribution from shareholders?

47 | Physicians of America

Congratulations. You've made it through the book. In this last section, we will look at some real-world examples. We will see how you might apply these principles and techniques in your own practice.

Physicians of America

Physicians of America is a privately-held, three-physician primary care group. They employ a radiation technologist, a medical technologist, one receptionist, one licensed nurse practitioner, three registered nurses, and one office manager. They have their own lab and radiology equipment because they want to provide easy and fast testing for their patients. Their financial reports are listed in Figure 6.1 and Figure 6.2. We will refer to these two reports and the accompanying operational data to illustrate important ratios and metrics you might want to examine on a regular basis.

The physicians of POA have been provided with the following income statement, shown in Figure 6.1, and the balance sheets in Figure 6.2. Let's take a look at how we might calculate some of the ratios we discussed earlier.

Figure 6.1 - Physicians of America Income Statements

Income Statement

		12/31/14		12/31/15
Gross Charges				
Professional Service Charges	$	1,139,223	$	1,275,745
Orthopedic Charges	$	9,101	$	8,143
Injection Charges	$	101,941	$	105,328
Immunization Charges	$	147,206	$	104,298
Procedure Charges	$	115,860	$	115,725
Laboratory Charges	$	728,329	$	711,383
Radiology Charges	$	122,113	$	125,539
Hospital Charges	$	84,383	$	124,821
Nursing Home Charges	$	20,061	$	46,825
Miscellaneous Charges	$	3,375	$	2,364
Gross Charges Total	$	2,471,593	$	2,620,171
Contractual Adjustments	$	(1,121,820)	$	(1,066,797)
Net Medical Charges	$	1,349,773	$	1,553,374
Capitation Revenue	$	121,245	$	138,231
Other Operating Income	$	65,262	$	43,901
Adj to Cash Collections	$	259,478	$	160,886
Total Net Revenue	$	1,795,757	$	1,896,391
Expenses				
Total Personnel Expense	$	599,496	$	731,954
Total Computer Expense	$	21,929	$	15,128
Total Radiology Expense	$	28,984	$	28,214
Total Laboratory Exp	$	89,068	$	91,885
Total Building Exp	$	232,875	$	235,926
Total Supplies Expense	$	114,888	$	110,688
Total Operating Expenses	$	1,087,240	$	1,213,795
Total Furn / Equip Exp	$	7,684	$	9,805
Total Purchased Svcs	$	29,845	$	21,785
Total EE Related Svcs	$	22,016	$	25,963
Total Gen & Adm Exp	$	41,272	$	41,886
Non-Op Rev/Exp	$	71,493	$	44,702
Total Overhead	$	172,310	$	144,141
Total Expenses	$	1,259,550	$	1,357,936
Net Profit	$	536,207	$	538,455

Figure 6.2 - Physicians of America Balance Sheets

Balance Sheet

	12/31/14	12/31/15
Current Assets		
Cash in Bank	$ 23,139	$ 28,602
Savings Acct	$ 59,725	$ 61,792
Patients Receivable	$ 251,944	$ 284,160
Accounts Receivable-Bldg	$ 95,065	$ 95,065
Receipts not Posted	$ (164)	$ (164)
Pre-paid Insurance		
Investment Receivables	$ 2,600	$ 1,200
Total Current Assets	$ 432,309	$ 470,655
Fixed Assets		
Furniture & Fixtures	$ 219,624	$ 219,624
Software	$ 64,093	$ 64,093
Accumulated Depreciation	$ (266,147)	$ (280,246)
Total Property & Equipment	$ 17,570	$ 3,471
Other Assets		
Organizational Costs	$ 3,406	$ 3,406
Accumulated Amortization	$ (3,406)	$ (3,406)
Utility Deposit	$ 3,215	$ 3,215
Inv-TI	$ 5,111	$ 3,444
Total Other Assets	$ 8,326	$ 6,659
Total Assets	$ 458,205	$ 480,786
Current Liabilities		
Loans Payable—Line of Credit	$ 44,274	$ 113,702
Loans Payable—Malpractice		
Loans Payable—Furniture, Furnishings, and Equipment	$ 31,341	$ 14,714
FUTA Tax Payable	$ 31	$ 32
SUTA Tax Payable	$ 40	$ 39
Total Current Liabilities	$ 75,686	$ 128,487
Deferred Revenue		
Deferred Accounts Receivable	$ 254,883	$ 253,635
Total Liabilities	$ 330,569	$ 382,122
Members' Capital		
Retained Earnings	$ 53,700	$ 50,557
Members' Capital Accounts	$ 25,470	$ 57,660
Members' Curr Yr Capital Contrib.	$ 1,500	$ 3,613
General Draws	$ (430,445)	$ (519,886)
Draws—Health, Dental	$ (14,574)	$ (9,340)
Draws—Life & Disability Ins.	$ (6,128)	$ (3,103)
Draws—401(K) Deferral	$ (38,093)	$ (19,292)
Current Yr Net Income	$ 536,206	$ 538,455
Total Members' Capital	$ 127,636	$ 98,664
Total Liabilities & Capital	$ 458,205	$ 480,786

Current Ratio

Dr. Stone is worried about the level of debt the company is carrying. He has a feeling they have been taking on too much debt. After looking at the reports, Dr. Stone calculates the current ratio for the last two years. He discovers that the current ratio has declined over the course of a year. It's still above 1.0 which is good, but not as high as it was. He wonders, "Why? What decisions or events occurred to alter this ratio?"

$$\text{Current ratio} = \frac{\text{Current assets}}{\text{Current liabilities}}$$

$$\text{Current ratio FY14} = \frac{\$432,309}{\$75,868}$$

$$\text{Current ratio FY14} = 5.71$$

$$\text{Current ratio FY15} = \frac{\$470,655}{\$128,487}$$

$$\text{Current ratio FY15} = 3.66$$

He notices that the company's total liabilities grew by about $51,000, most of which is accounted for by the line of credit, which has increased by $50,000. He also sees that the A/R has grown by $33,000. That might account for the use of the line of credit. Even though the assets grew by $38,000, the growth of the liabilities is concerning. With changes in healthcare, patients are having a harder time paying their portions of their medical bills. Also, it would appear the physicians took an additional $12,000 out of equity. Basically, they paid themselves the cash and borrowed it. Interesting….

Working Capital

Dr. Stone is also concerned about the company's cash flow. He has heard that CMS might perform a review of their charts. During the review period, CMS won't pay the group any money, yet POA will keep seeing CMS patients. He's concerned about two things.

First, how much of their practice does CMS account for? Second, can they afford such an event in his group? Do they have enough working capital to cope with such an audit?

Working capital = Current assets - Current liabilities

Working capital FY14 = $432,309 - $75,686 = $356,623

Working capital FY14 = $356,623

Working capital FY15 = $470,655 - $128,487 = $342,168

Working capital FY15 = $342,168

He discovers working capital has decreased by $14,000 over the last year. They have a nice cushion of $342,000, but it has shrunk. He also discovers that CMS accounts for about 32% of their business. If that revenue dries up for three months, what will happen?

A Revenue Stream Dries Up Temporarily

So what will happen if CMS withholds payments for three months? To begin with, we need to make a few assumptions. First, we know CMS represents 32% of all patient visits. What hasn't been provided is the percentage of the revenue that CMS represents. We know they are POA's lowest payers, so it is safe to assume that their payments represent at most 32% of our collections. We will also assume that CMS patient volume doesn't change and neither does the patient volume from other third-party payers.

Can the clinic survive? Sure. Do they have the cash? Maybe. The question is, which of their current assets can they liquidate to cover the shortfall? Are those assets needed for the delivery of patient care? How much of those assets is money they are owed anyway? Will they need to borrow the money until the CMS payments come in? After examining their balance sheet, it doesn't appear that the assets can cover the shortage. It looks like POA will need to secure a line of credit to make payroll and pay their bills until the audit is completed. POA will need to find a way to account for a $33,000 loss each month. This is shown in Figure 6.3.

Figure 6.3 - Effect of a Slow Payer

	Assumptions	Current Situation	Month 1	Month 2	Month 3
CMS % of revenue			32%	32%	32%
Visits per month	880	880	880	880	880
Revenue per visit	$ 163	$ 143,440	$ 97,539	$ 97,539	$ 97,539
Variable costs per visit	$ 120	$ 105,600	$ 105,600	$ 105,600	$ 105,600
Contribution margin	$ 43	$ 37,840	$ (8,061)	$ (8,061)	$ (8,061)
Fixed costs	$ 25,000	$ 25,000	$ 25,000	$ 25,000	$ 25,000
Net income		$ 12,840	$ (33,061)	$ (33,061)	$ (33,061)
Total shortfall in cash			$ (33,061)	$ (66,122)	$ (99,182)

There are a few lessons to learned from this example. First, make certain you've got cash reserves in case of an emergency. That's why looking at your working capital is handy. Maybe you don't bonus out as much cash, or maybe you put it into other liquid assets. (There is a much larger discussion regarding taxes and cash, when to pay it out, etc. Discuss this with your accountants!)

Second, always have a line of credit or business loan available. Get your credit in place before you need it, not when you need it. When the economy took a turn for the worse in 2008, Ford didn't need TARP funds because they already had lines of credit in place. You can see why proper planning and capital financing is so important to get you through the lean times.

You might be wondering how Dr. Stone arrived at his revenue and costs number. Let's take a look at that right now.

Costs

For the past twelve months, the clinic has been collecting operational data. They know how much they spend each month and have guessed at their monthly revenue. It's a guess because they use a cash-based accounting system and it isn't that sophisticated. But they do have their expenses, or costs, for each month, so they can use their activity levels and cost data to create a model. The raw data is shown in Figure 6.4.

Figure 6.4 - Physicians of America Operational Data

Month	Visits	Expenses
Jan	540	$ 89,740
Feb	553	$ 90,300
Mar	683	$ 105,900
Apr	715	$ 111,050
May	644	$ 103,470
Jun	624	$ 99,380
Jul	657	$ 105,030
Aug	689	$ 106,680
Sep	676	$ 107,120
Oct	546	$ 91,270
Nov	540	$ 90,740
Dec	624	$ 99,880

Using Excel or any other spreadsheet, Dr. Stone plotted the data on a graph like Figure 6.5. Using the handy features in Excel, he was able to find a trend line or do a quick regression on the data set.

Figure 6.5 - Physicians of America Expense Graph

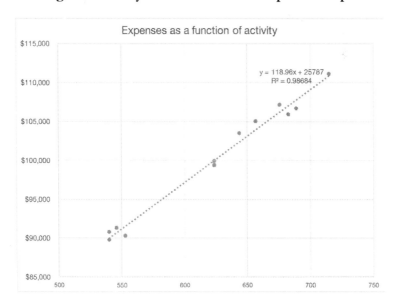

The program also calculates the equation for us. The variable costs, or dependent variable, is y. The equation is $y=118.96x + 25787$. According to this equation, their fixed costs are $25,787 and their variable costs are $118.96 per each patient visit. Dr. Stone knows this is only a model with error, but it is a good starting point for projecting and budgeting. He is aware that these are estimates and guesses. They aren't hard and fast numbers but serve as a guide in the decision-making process.

Using the cost data, Dr. Stone can calculate the revenue estimates. He decides to use a simple method of blending all of the revenue together as a charge per visit, a weighted average of revenue per patient visit. In doing so, he discovers that on average they collect about $163 for each patient visit to the clinic.

"You've got to spend money to make money."

Dr. Martin has a cousin who works as an internet marketer. He is a guru of online marketing and has been telling Dr. Martin that his company can easily boost their patient volume by about 10%. The fee is only $4,000 per month. Dr. Martin is smart and decides to put pen to paper and run the numbers. (She's smart because she read this book on the advice of Dr. Stone!) Together with the office manager, she compiles the data in Figure 6.6.

Figure 6.6 - Current State of Physicians of America

	Current
Visits/month	886
Revenue/month	$ 144,208
Variable costs/month	$ 105,399
Contribution margin	$ 38,809
Fixed costs	$ 25,787
Net income	$ 13,022

Next, she creates a model of the proposed marketing plan. She's decided to classify the marketing cost as a fixed cost because it will be for one year and will not change with the clinic's activity. The proposed state is shown in Figure 6.7.

Figure 6.7 - Proposed State of Physicians of America

	Current	Proposed
Visits/month	886	975
Revenue/month	$ 144,208	$ 158,694
Variable costs/month	$ 105,399	$ 115,986
Contribution margin	$ 38,809	$ 42,708
Fixed costs	$ 25,787	$ 29,787
Net income	$ 13,022	$ 12,921

She notices that she will either break even or lose a little money on the marketing campaign. She realizes these are just projections, so an allowance for error is needed. She wonders just how many patients she will need to see each month for the marketing campaign to break even. Using Excel's Goal Seek tool, she runs an analysis and finds they will need to see 980 patients each month. The results are shown in Figure 6.8.

Figure 6.8 - Needed Visits of Physicians of America

	Current	Proposed	Needed
Visits/month	886	975	980
Revenue/month	$ 144,208	$ 158,694	$ 159,508
Variable costs/month	$ 105,399	$ 115,986	$ 116,581
Contribution margin	$ 38,809	$ 42,708	$ 42,927
Fixed costs	$ 25,787	$ 29,787	$ 29,787
Net income	$ 13,022	$ 12,921	$ 13,140

So, it's not too far off, but can they handle that volume? Do they have the staff for it? Does her costing data account for overtime for her employees? How late into the day will the clinic need to operate?

Will they need to cut visit times down to stay within their normal operating hours? If so, what will that do to their quality of care and patient satisfaction?

There are still many questions that need to be answered before she can bring this idea to the partners. However, she knows $4,000 per month is just too high. Perhaps he can give her a "good cousin" discount that will help her be profitable—maybe $3,000 per month. At that price, the clinic might earn around $1,000 more each month if the volume grows by the promised 10%. But is it worth it? To break even on the year of marketing, the clinic will need to grow by 8% at a $3,000 per month marketing expense. Figure 6.9 shows this analysis.

Figure 6.9 - Needed Visits Scenario 2 of Physicians of America

	Current		Proposed		Needed	
Visits/month		886		975		955
Revenue/month	$	144,208	$	158,694	$	155,439
Variable costs/month	$	105,399	$	115,986	$	113,607
Contribution margin	$	38,809	$	42,708	$	41,832
Fixed costs	$	25,787	$	28,787	$	28,787
Net income	$	13,022	$	13,921	$	13,045

Everyone Wants a Discount

Dan, the office manager, received a letter from Blue Cross Blue Shield of their intent to continue contracting with POA for services. However, since the current contract expires soon, the powers that be at BCBS would like a little bigger discount. They claim costs are rising and they simply cannot afford to pay their current rates. Therefore, they claim they need an additional 5% discount off their current rates. Dan is planning to share this letter with the three physicians at the next board meeting. But first, he thought he would do a little analysis for them.

Let's assume the blended unit is $163. Their base unit is $223 per visit. BCBS gets a 14.6% discount in the current agreement. That makes their net collection per visit $190. Another 5% reduction would take their payment to POA down to $179. Their variable costs are $120 per visit, so they will still make $59 less their fixed costs per BCBS patient visit. If historical trends continue, they will witness a $20,000 decrease in revenue from BCBS alone over the course of a year. By understanding how to interpret financial statements and how to calculate their costs, they are better prepared and informed before they sit down at the negotiation table.

What If the Payer is Always Late?

What happens if one of your payers takes more time to pay you? Can you deal with that? You would perform the same analysis as you did in the example above. Look at your projected revenue and estimated costs. If you can take the hit, that is one thing, but *should* you is another. Examine your contract closely. All of your contracts should be kept in a file and reviewed on a regular basis. Don't rely on your billing company to do this for you. Their job is to collect money for you. You should review the contracts regularly and be aware of any hidden clauses or surprises. It's been said the hard part of a deal isn't the negotiation, but rather the actual performance of the contract.

Where Does Our Money Come From?

That's an excellent question. Where does POA's money come from? It's important to know and understand where your revenue is coming from. Let's look at their revenue distribution for FY14 in Figure 6.10.

Figure 6.10 - Service Line Analysis

2014

Gross Charges

Professional Service Charges	$	1,139,223	46.09%
Orthopedic Charges	$	9,101	0.37%
Injection Charges	$	101,941	4.12%
Immunization Charges	$	147,206	5.96%
Procedure Charges	$	115,860	4.69%
Laboratory Charges	$	728,329	29.47%
Radiology Charges	$	122,113	4.94%
Hospital Charges	$	84,383	3.41%
Nursing Home Charges	$	20,061	0.81%
Miscellanous Charges	$	3,375	0.14%
Gross Charges Total	$	2,471,593	

Here we see that 46% of their revenue comes from seeing patients. Almost 30% of their revenue comes from laboratory testing. Radiological studies account for about 5% of their charges. This is important to know as payers kick around ideas of cutting fees or stopping payment altogether. Let's suppose a payer in your state is toying with the idea of not paying for practice-owned labs and instead contracts that out to a local hospital and laboratory. What happens to your revenue? Can you afford the cut?

Putting it All Together

I hope you are beginning to see the importance of becoming a financially intelligent physician. The examples in this chapter are real-life applications and issues faced by some of my physician friends. They are illustrations of the concepts discussed earlier in the book. As you begin to invest in yourself with knowledge, analyzing financial reports and making decisions will become easier and easier for you. It is similar to practicing medicine for years. With repeated practice, you become better and stronger clinically. The same will happen when you begin to practice financial analysis on a regular basis.

48

What I Was Really Given

At first, I wasn't going to put the original reports in this book. But the more I thought about it, the more I felt the need to illustrate an important lesson. When you review the above financial reports, what stands out to you? What appears to be a little bit off? Where is the cash? Why is it negative? How does cash go negative?

It's okay if you didn't see the negative cash balance in one account when you first looked at the report. An important lesson here is to always look for the cash balance. So many issues are created and solved with cash that you really need to know your daily cash position.

Use the checklist I provided in Chapter 46 as a guide. The real reports are shown in Figures 6.11 and 6.12. Start at the top of the report and work your way down to the bottom. Don't skip to the bottom line—try to understand what decisions have affected it.

Some line items are abbreviated and may not make sense. If you don't understand an accountant's particular abbreviation, ask for clarification. Also note, they aren't always the best at spelling or grammar.

Figure 6.11 - Real Income Statement from Private Practice Clinic

Income Statement
December 31, 2014

Gross Charges:

Professional Service Charges	1,139,223
Orthopedic Charges	9,101
Injection Charges	101,941
Immunization Charges	147,206
Procedure Charges	115,860
Laboratory Charges	728,329
Radiology Charges	122,113
Hospital Charges	84,383
Nursing Home Charges	20,061
Miscellaneous Charges	3,375
Gross Charges Total:	**2,471,593**

Contractual Adjustments:

Other Contractual Adjustments	(65,177)
Aetna Adjustments	(19,267)
BC/BS Adjustments	(171,064)
Cigna Adjustments	(7,651)
Coventry Adjustments	(123,789)
Medicare Adjustments	(324,835)
PHS Adjustments	(72,798)
PPK Adjustments	(97,514)
United Adjustments	(83,310)
WPPA Adjustments	(8,749)
Non-contractual Adjustments	(36,277)
Pre-Paid Contract Adj. - PPK	(73,886)
Refunds	(37,503)
Contractual Adjustments Total:	**(1,121,820)**
Net Medical Charges:	**1,349,773**
Capitation Revenue	121,245
Other Operating Income	65,262
Adj to Cash Collections	259,478
Total Net Revenue:	**1,795,757**

Expenses

Total Professional Exp	189,703
Total EE Exp	398,454
Drugs & Meds	86,116
Medical Supp	15,030
Office Supplies	6,751
Laundry & Linen	4,485
Janitorial Supp	2,506
Total Supplies Expense	114,887
Comp Equip < $500	346
Comp Equip Maint	20,894
Comp Equip / Dep Exp	689
Total Computer Expense	21,928
Radiology Supplies	0
Outside Radiology Fees	21,008
Radiology Equip Lease/Rent	0
Radiology Equip Maint	7,754
Other Radiology Exp	222
Total Radiology Expense	28,984
Lab Supplies	49,250
Outside Lab Fees	21,051
Lab Equip Lease / Rent	9,812
Lab Equip Maint	2,438
Other Lab Exp	6,517
Total Laboratory Exp	89,069
Bio-Hazard Waste	3,930
Building Lease	220,391
Janitorial Services	8,554
Total Building Exp	232,875
Furn / Equip Lease	3,151
Property Tax Furn / Equip	278
Insurance Furn / Equip	1,779
Maint / Repairs Furn / Equip	2,218
Small Tools & Equip	258
Total Furn / Equip Exp	7,685

Legal Fees	2,333
Accounting Fees	2,195
Collection Svcs	0
Other Purchased Svcs	25,267
Transcription Svcs	0
Storage Exp	50
Total Purchased Svcs	29,846
Recruitment	231
Employee Relations	533
Prof Liability Insurance	21,252
Total EE Related Svcs	22,016
Telephone Exp	10,933
Prof Listings / Promo	12,095
Postage & Freight	8,095
Bank Fees	9,241
Books, Subscrip, Etc.	890
Other G&A Exp	18
Total Gen & Adm Exp	41,272
Total Operating Exp	1,176,718
Total Non-Op Rev/Exp	71,493
Total Physician Sal/Ben	11,339
Total Expenses	1,259,551
Net Profit	536,206

Figure 6.12 - Real Balance Sheet from Private Practice Clinic

Balance Sheet
December 31, 2014

Current Assets	
Cash in Bank	(383.78)
Savings Acct	59,725
Patients Receivable	251,944
Accounts Receivable-Bldg	95,065
Receipts not Posted	(164)
Pre-Paid Insurance	
Investment Receivables	2,600
Total Current Assets	**408,786**
Fixed Assets	
Furniture & Fixtures	219,624
Software	64,093
Accumulated Depreciation	(266,147)
Total Property & Equipment	**17,570**
Other Assets	
Organizational Costs	3,406
Accumulated Amortization	(3,406)
Utility Deposit	3,215
Inv-TI	5,111
Total Other Assets	**8,326**
Total Assets	**434,682**
Current Liabilities	
Loans Payable—Line Of Credit	44,274
Loans Payable—Malpractice	
Loans Payable—Furniture, Furnishings, and Equipme	31,341
FUTA Tax Payable	31
SUTA Tax Payable	40
Total Current Liabilities	**75,686**
Deferred Revenue	
Deferred Accounts Receivable	254,883
Total Liabilities	**330,569**
Members' Capital	
Retained Earnings	53,700
Members' Capital Accounts	25,470
Members' Curr Yr Capital Contrib.	1,500
General Draws	(453,968)
Draws—Health, Dental	(14,574)
Draws—Life & Disability Ins.	(6,128)
Draws—401(K) Deferral	(38,093)
Current Yr Net Income	536,206
Total Members' Capital	**104,113**
Total Liabilities & Capital	**434,682**

Closing Remarks

I hope you've found at least a few items in this book helpful. It is my hope and desire that you've expanded your knowledge of finance and accounting. I trust you are now more adept at reading the financial statements of your practice.

Making the proper financial decisions can only begin once we have a solid understanding of the story the numbers are telling us. Always ask questions when you don't understand something. If the answer doesn't make sense, keep asking questions. Listen to that little voice in your head. Don't be afraid to request financial reports or explanations or more in-depth analyses. Treat your practice as a patient.

Please feel free to give me feedback about the book. I would love to hear how this book has helped you improve your practice. Send me an email at david@davidnorrismdmba.com and let me know. Visit learn.davidnorrismdmba.com for my online training courses.

Sincerely,
David

Appendix

My Favorite Online Resources

Here is a list of some of my favorite websites and online tools if you are looking to learn more about how to apply the concepts in this book:

- Investopedia (http://www.investopedia.com)
- Accounting Coach (http://www.accountingcoach.com)
- Finance Formulas (http://www.financeformulas.net)
- Business Dictionary (http://www.businessdictionary.com/)
- Accounting Tools (http://www.accountingtools.com)
- Investing Answers (http://www.investinganswers.com)

About the Author

David J Norris, MD, MBA is a practicing cardiac anesthesiologist in Wichita, KS. He graduated from the University of Kansas School of Medicine and completed his residency in anesthesiology and fellowship in cardiac anesthesiology at Vanderbilt University Medical Center.

After receiving financial reports for his group, he realized he lacked the fundamental knowledge required to use these reports. This prompted him to obtain a Masters of Business Administration from Wichita State University. He now travels across the country teaching the fundamentals of business to others in healthcare. Dr. Norris speaks at conferences, private training workshops, and works onsite with clients to help them improve their business knowledge.

Dr. Norris is still clinically active with the same group he joined in 2004. He is happily married to Megan and has two children, Jacob and Adelle. He enjoys writing, teaching, and flying.

Made in the USA
Middletown, DE
26 January 2019